LABOR UNIONS

AND THE

ECONOMIC PERFORMANCE

OF

FIRMS

Barry T. Hirsch

1991

W. E. UPJOHN INSTITUTE for Employment Research
Kalamazoo, Michigan

Library of Congress Cataloging-in-Publication Data

Hirsch, Barry T., 1949-
    Labor unions and the economic performance of firms / Barry T.
Hirsch.
        p.   cm.
    Includes bibliographical references and index.
    ISBN 0-88099-109-7   (hardcover : acid-free). — ISBN 0-88099-110-0
(paper : acid-free)
        1. Trade-unions—Economic aspects—United States. 2. Profit—
United States. 3. Capital investments—United States.
    4. Research, Industrial—United States. 5. Industrial productivity—
United States.   I. Title
    HD6508.H483 1991
    331.88'0973—dc20   91-2576
                                                                    CIP

THE INSTITUTE, a nonprofit research organization, was established on July 1, 1945. It is an activity of the W. E. Upjohn Unemployment Trustee Corporation, which was formed in 1932 to administer a fund set aside by the late Dr. W. E. Upjohn for the purpose of carrying on ''research into the causes and effects of unemployment and measures for the alleviation of unemployment.''

Cover design by J.R. Underhill
Index prepared by Shirley Kessel
Printed in the United States of America

THE AUTHOR

Barry Hirsch is Professor of Economics at The Florida State University. He is the author (along with John Addison) of *The Economic Analysis of Unions: New Approaches and Evidence,* and of numerous articles in leading general and labor economics journals. He has broad research interests in the area of labor economics; recent work has focused on the relationship between labor unions and firm economic behavior and performance. He received his B.A. and Ph.D. from the University of Virginia.

POLICY SUMMARY

This monograph examines the relationship between labor unions and the economic performance and behavior of U.S. firms. A model of union rent-seeking is developed in which unions capture a share of the quasi-rents that make up the normal return to investment in long-lived capital and research and development (R&D). In response to union rent-seeking, firms adjust their investment in vulnerable tangible and intangible capital. In order to examine empirically union effects on firm performance, a survey was conducted to collect information on the extent of collective bargaining coverage among publicly traded manufacturing firms. Data from the union survey are matched with firm and industry data to form a large panel data set of firms for the 1968-1980 period. These data permit a relatively detailed examination of the relationship of unionization with firm profitability and market value, investment in physical capital and R&D, productivity, and productivity growth.

Firm-level union coverage is found to vary substantially both across and within industries. Evidence is provided showing that companies with extensive unionization had lower rates of profit, market value, capital investment, and R&D investment than did similar nonunion firms and those firms with limited collective bargaining coverage. Returns to physical capital and R&D and the disequilibrium returns associated with demand shifts, rather than monopoly profits associated with market structure, appear to provide the primary sources for union gains. Although union-nonunion differences in profitability and investment are large on average, there is substantial variability in estimated union effects across industries. Econometric evidence on productivity and productivity growth differences between union and nonunion companies is fragile and allows few clear-cut inferences to be drawn. The recent contraction in the size of the union sector, it is argued, resulted in part from the long-run response by firms to union rent-seeking, and was inevitable given the relatively poor profit performance, diminished market value, and low investment by unionized companies during the 1970s.

CONTENTS

TABLES

FIGURES

1
Introduction

During the 1970s and 1980s, there was a substantial decline in the relative importance of labor unions and of manufacturing production in the United States. Over this same period, a marked slowdown in aggregate wage and productivity growth drew increased attention from policymakers and economists. Only recently have researchers focused attention on the effects of labor unions on economic performance and examined the relationship between economic performance and declining union membership. This study analyzes in detail union effects on profitability, investment behavior, productivity, and productivity growth during the 1970s, based on new evidence collected on union membership at the firm level.

The decline in U.S. unionization has been greeted with unrestrained glee by many business groups and with grave concern (often coupled with resignation) by union supporters. The extent of the union decline is evinced by statistics on union membership and representation elections. Union density, measured by the percentage of nonagricultural employment comprised of union members, fell from 30 percent in 1970, to 23 percent in 1980, and to 17 percent by 1987 (19 percent were *covered* by collective bargaining agreements during 1987).[1] The survey of publicly traded U.S. manufacturing companies conducted for this study (see chapter 3) finds that among 452 companies providing information for both 1977 and 1987, collective bargaining coverage declined from 30.5 percent in 1977 to 25.0 percent in 1987. Current Population Survey (CPS) data on individual manufacturing sector workers in 1987 indicates that 24.7 percent were covered by a collective bargaining agreement (U.S. Bureau of the Census 1989, table 684). Data on new union organizing reveal a similar pattern over time, the ratio of union representation elections and new workers organized to total employment both falling sharply since the 1950s.[2] Although it is difficult to predict future levels of union representation, Freeman (1985, p. 49) calculated a long-run, steady-state

1

union coverage density of about 10 percent in the private sector, based on trends in new organizing and coverage loss (decay) through 1980. Subsequent organizing and decay trends now suggest steady-state levels of private sector union coverage of less than 5 percent (Freeman 1988; Chaison and Dhavale 1990).

Explanations for the decline in unionism abound, although the relative importance of contributing factors remains very much in doubt (see, for example, Dickens and Leonard 1985; Hirsch and Addison 1986, chap. 3; Freeman 1988; Reder 1988). The explanation most commonly proffered is that "structural" changes in the U.S. economy have led to declines in unionization. It is argued that employment has declined in historically highly unionized sectors of the economy (e.g., production jobs in manufacturing), whereas job growth has occurred in nonproduction jobs in the largely nonunion service sector. Complementary explanations include increased foreign competition impacting most directly the goods-producing sectors of the economy, deregulation in highly unionized transportation and communication industries, more rapid job growth in low-union regions of the country, increased entry of women into low-union sectors of the labor market, and less favorable attitudes toward unions exhibited by management, workers, legislatures, and administrative and judicial authorities.

Recent studies have challenged purely structural explanations for declining unionism. Linneman and Wachter (1986) provide evidence that within 1-digit industries, declines in employment from 1973-1984 are restricted almost entirely to union workers while, in contrast, nonunion employment grew in almost all sectors. They calculate union premiums in each industry, relative to an "opportunity cost" wage in growing (primarily nonunion) sectors of the economy. Union premiums are found to have increased over this period and Linneman and Wachter conclude that much of the decline in union employment was in response to higher union wage premiums. Linneman, Wachter, and Carter (1990), who provide more recent and detailed evidence, reach an identical conclusion. Likewise, Freeman (1985; 1988) is skeptical of the structural explanation, noting that Canada has not had such significant declines in unionism, despite similar structural changes. Freeman links the decline in unionism to increased management opposition (evidenced primarily by increased unfair labor practice charges) resulting, he argues, from an increased union wage premium and less favorable NLRB rulings. Blanchflower and Freeman (forthcoming) utilize international data and conclude that in the United States the union wage premium is larger, and decline in union density greater, than in other OECD countries.

This monograph examines a related explanation for union decline. A model of union rent-seeking is described in which unions capture some share of the quasi-rents that make up the normal return to investment in long-lived capital and in research and development (R&D). In response, firms rationally reduce their investment in vulnerable tangible and intangible capital. Contraction of the union sector, it is argued, has resulted in part from the long-run response by firms to union rent-seeking, and was inevitable given the relatively poor economic performance and prospects among unionized companies during the 1970s. Specifically, companies with extensive unionization are found to have had lower rates of profit, market value, capital investment, and R&D investment than similar companies whose workers had limited collective bargaining coverage.

The union rent-seeking framework introduced in this monograph contrasts with the traditional on-the-demand curve model. In the traditional model, union monopoly power in the labor market is viewed as changing relative factor prices through its ability to raise union compensation above competitive levels. In response to a higher wage, union firms move up and along their labor-demand curve by decreasing employment, hiring higher-quality workers, and increasing the ratio of capital to labor. Total investment in innovative activity and labor-saving capital can increase or decrease owing to offsetting substitution and scale effects.

The traditional model may be inadequate in this instance for at least two reasons. First, settlements off-the-labor-demand curve, with lower wages and greater employment than would obtain in the on-the-demand curve model, are preferred by both the union and management. If settlements are not on-the-labor-demand curve, the effect of unions on factor mix cannot be predicted in straightforward fashion. A second shortcoming is the traditional model's characterization of union wage increases as exogenous or independent of factor price changes. In the rent-seeking framework, union wage premiums are viewed as levying a tax on firm earnings. The union tax is not viewed as an independent factor price change but, rather, as an *outcome* made possible by both union power in the labor market and the presence of firm quasi-rents.

Implications of the rent-seeking model differ from the traditional on-the-demand curve model. Firms may be less rather than more likely to commit to tangible and intangible capital investments that are relatively long-lived and nontransferable, since such investments will face high union tax rates. Long-run implications deriving from the union rent-seeking model include the possibility of lower rates of profit and capital investment, decreases in R&D and other innovative activities, and slower productivity and output growth. These possibilities are explored in subsequent chapters.

Empirical work in this monograph builds on a rapidly growing literature examining union effects on profitability and productivity, and a more limited body of evidence examining union effects on firm investment and productivity growth. Studies examining union effects on profits almost universally find that unions decrease profitability. This conclusion holds for studies using industries, firms, or lines of business as the unit of observation; for models where the profitability measures are industry price-cost margins, firm rates of return to capital or sales, Tobin's q or other market value measures, or stock market value changes in response to union "events"; for simultaneous equation as well as single equation models; and regardless of the time period under study.

Despite the consensus that profitability is lower in unionized settings, there is disagreement as to the magnitude of the profit reduction and the sources from which union gains are obtained. Economists are understandably skeptical that large profit differentials can survive in a competitive economy, notwithstanding the sizable union-nonunion profit differences found in the empirical literature. Unfortunately, little attention has been given to the sources from which unions appropriate rents. Several studies conclude that unions reduce profits primarily in highly concentrated industries and that monopoly power provides the primary source for union compensation gains. Other studies call this conclusion into question and argue that returns from firm-specific R&D capital and weak foreign competition are more likely sources for union gains.

Little attention has been given to union-nonunion differences in investment behavior. The union rent-seeking model predicts that unionized firms invest less in highly taxed investment paths than do similar nonunion firms. The small number of previous studies examining union effects on firm investment behavior provide support for the union rent-seeking model. Unionized companies invest less in physical capital and R&D than do similar nonunion companies, and the level of innovative activity appears to be decreased by union coverage. If unionized firms invest less in tangible and intangible capital, over the long run they should have slower growth in output and employment. While there is surprisingly little research on this latter topic, studies do suggest, however, that unionization has produced significantly slower employment growth (Linneman, Wachter, and Carter 1990; Leonard forthcoming) and, perhaps, weaker sales (output) growth (Clark 1984; Freeman and Medoff 1984).

Union effects on productivity have received considerable attention since the appearance of the study by Brown and Medoff (1978), which concluded that union establishments are about 20 percent more productive than similar nonunion establishments, after accounting for differences in capital intensity and labor quality. Considerable methodological reservations attach to this and other studies in this literature, however. The fuller body of empirical evidence does not suggest a sizable union productivity effect, nor are large productivity effects consistent with empirical evidence on profitability and employment (Addison and Hirsch 1989).

The link between unions and productivity *growth* is rather opaque. There are numerous studies examining total factor productivity growth, many of which include industry union density as a control variable. These studies generally find productivity growth lower among firms and industries with high union densities, but this result is suspect given the data and econometric limitations of these studies. The rent-seeking model implies, however, that even if unionism has no direct effect on productivity growth, it may affect it indirectly via union effects on growth-enhancing investments in physical and R&D capital.

A serious limitation of much of the previous empirical research on unions and firm performance has been the difficulty in obtaining firm-level measures of union coverage. In order to examine union effects on firm performance, 1977 union data from the survey conducted in this study were matched to company and industry data on a panel of U.S. manufacturing firms over the 1968-1980 period. Use of this data set facilitates a detailed examination of the relationship between unionization and firm performance.

Union coverage data for 1987 were also collected. Because of limitations on other firm and industry data available at the time this study was conducted, the 1987 data were not used to analyze union effects on firm performance. The data, however, provide direct evidence on the magnitude of firm-specific changes in union coverage between 1977 and 1987 (chapter 3). No such information is publicly available.

In the following chapters, theory and evidence on the relationship between unions, investment, and economic performance are provided. Chapter 2 presents a theoretical development of the union rent-seeking model, in which union effects on profitability, the level and mix of tangible and intangible capital investments, factor usage, and productivity growth are examined. In chapter 3, detailed discussion of the union coverage survey is provided. Chapter 4 provides the modeling and estimation of union effects on firm profitability and market value. Firm investment behavior is examined in chapter 5, while productivity and productivity growth are the focus of chapter 6. Chapters 4, 5, and 6 each contain a brief survey of previous research in the area under study. A summary and evaluation are provided in chapter 7.

NOTES

1. Data for 1970 and 1980 are from Troy and Sheflin (1985, table 3.41). Figures for 1987 are derived from the Current Population Survey (U.S. Bureau of the Census 1989, table 684). Although the former source calculates figures based on union-reported dues, and the latter on surveys of individuals, figures from the two surveys are very close during years in which both report union density. Private sector union membership density is substantially lower than economywide density. Estimates of union membership and contract coverage by detailed industry and geographic area are provided in Curme, Hirsch, and Macpherson (1990).

2. Election data are summarized in NLRB Annual Reports (these reports have not appeared regularly during the 1980s) and are made available on data tapes. There was a particularly sharp and permanent drop in union organizing activity between 1981 and 1982; the average 1982-1987 level of organizing is about half the 1975-1981 level (Chaison and Dhavale 1990, table 1, p. 369).

2
Union Rent-Seeking
and the
Economic Performance of Firms

A firm and labor union engage in a long-run bilateral relationship in which both parties have market power and receive economic quasi-rents from their mutual relationship. Quasi-rents are the returns accruing to previously "installed" physical, intangible, or human capital above those obtainable in the capital's best alternative use. Quasi-rents, therefore, are prevalent where physical capital or worker skills are specialized, long-lived, and costly to transfer to an alternative use. Although competitive labor market conditions heavily influence bargaining outcomes, both parties possess some degree of market power. On the one hand, U.S. labor law specifies that the union be the sole representative of covered workers and that the firm bargain in good faith with the union. Workers possess legally protected rights and firm-specific skills, and firms have made significant investments in human, physical, and intangible capital. Because it is costly for a firm to replace its unionized workforce, the union can appropriate some share of the firm's quasi-rents.

On the other hand, because workers possess nontransferable job skills (partially financed by workers) and face fixed costs of job switching, the firm may behave opportunistically and capture worker quasi-rents by paying workers only their current opportunity costs. Opportunistic behavior by the firm may be severely constrained, however, by the necessity to maintain a good reputation so as to attract quality workers in the future.

The existence of mutual rents in a long-run bargaining situation between firms and unions provides the setting for the union rent-seeking framework. Emphasis in this study is given to the ability of unions to appropriate firm quasi-rents. Below, union and firm behavior are analyzed and the implications for firms' investment behavior and economic performance are developed.

Union Behavior

Labor unions attempt to acquire gains for their members. Gains primarily take the form of wage increases, but may also be evinced by increases in nonwage compensation, improved employment security, changes in the wage distribution, and changes in the work environment and governance structure of firms. It is assumed that union leaders are responsive to the demands of the rank-and-file. Interest compatibility between agent (union leadership) and principals (rank-and-file) is enhanced by the necessity of union leaders to be reelected and to obtain majority approval of collective bargaining agreements. The simplest model of union behavior is the median voter model wherein preferences are well-ordered or "single peaked," so that individual preferences can be aggregated into ordered group preferences. Majority rule voting in this case produces a determinate and stable equilibrium. The median voter model predicts that union leaders propose and attempt to execute actions most consistent with the demands of union members with median or average preferences (Hirsch and Addison 1986, chap. 2; Farber 1986). While the assumptions of the median voter model are an overly simplistic *description* of union decisionmaking, the model provides a reasonable and appropriate framework for analyzing most union behavior.

Even if unions accurately represent current rank-and-file with median preferences, an inefficient output of union services results because the voting process does not readily permit weighting the intensity of preferences. More fundamental to the discussion that follows, if the concept of efficiency in union services is extended to include the preferences of potential or future union members, unions are likely to be "rationally myopic" in their actions, discounting too heavily long-run outcomes. Myopia results because incumbent union members do not have sufficient incentive to take into account the welfare of potential or future union members. The future is highly discounted because union members cannot sell their place in the union, members cannot transfer their membership as a bequest to children or friends, and the preferences of potential union members (i.e., qualified workers in the union queue) need not be taken into account. The discount rate at which unions evaluate long-run outcomes is increased further if the preferences of senior union members receive particularly large weights in the union calculus. It is argued below that the combination of union rent-seeking and myopia leads to important union effects on firm profitability and investment decisions, as well as other aspects of economic performance.

Union Rent-Seeking and Profitability

If unions reduce profitability significantly below a normal rate of return, survival rates for unionized firms (or lines of business within firms) will be lower than for their nonunion competitors. It is thus unlikely that unions can maintain large wage premiums in competitive industries with small stocks of specialized capital unless they also increase productivity significantly or organize industrywide in markets facing low product demand elasticities (due, say, to limited foreign competition). Industrywide unionism, in this case, acts much like a cartelizing device to lower output and raise price. The possibility that unions increase productivity sufficiently to offset higher wage costs is addressed subsequently.

Unions obtain compensation above competitive levels principally by sharing in a firm's monopoly returns and quasi-rents. Unionization is less likely to have an impact on firm survival and pricing-output decisions if excess returns accruing from imperfect product market competition provide the principal source for union gains. Although excess returns associated with market power may provide a target and potential source for union gains, it need not follow that unions can appropriate such returns. If the firm can continue operations during a sustained strike, or the resources that generate the monopoly returns can be costlessly transferred to a nonunion environment, the union may have relatively little bargaining power to tax monopoly returns. For example, a pharmaceutical company whose primary assets are highly valued patents may be able to sell (or license) these patents to another company. A strike threat by unionized production workers to shut down production would not be credible in this situation, since resources can be transferred at low cost to an equally valued alternative use. If a company's assets are costly to transfer and not equally valued elsewhere, returns associated with monopoly patents might better be treated as potentially appropriable quasi-rents.[1]

Quasi-rents are returns accruing to installed fixed-cost capital above its opportunity cost. For example, once investment in specialized plant or equipment has been made, a sizable reduction in the return stream from that capital will not cause it to be sold, scrapped, or shut down. Rather, assets will continue in use as long as they retain a return above that available in their best alternative use. Quasi-rents can, but need not, arise from imperfect competition; even with free entry and open competition, specialized assets create quasi-rents that make up the competitive return to investment. It is argued here that quasi-rents provide a primary source for union rent-seeking. And once a specialized asset is in place, union wage gains financed by appropriated returns are unlikely to affect that asset's use. In the long run, however, decreases in expected rates of return will cause union firms to invest less in long-lived specialized capital, until expected rates of return net of the union tax are equal to competitive market rates of return.

Effective union rent-seeking should lower firm profitability, regardless of whether union gains are at the expense of above-normal returns resulting from market power, or represent a share of the quasi-rents making up the normal returns to capital owners. Firm profitability can be represented by traditional accounting measures of earnings, market value measures (if the firm is publicly traded), or some combination of the two. The accounting profit measure utilized in subsequent empirical work is the rate of return on capital (earnings/capital stock). Accounting returns reflect historically observed performance, but do not directly reflect future performance or adjustments for risk. The return on equity (earnings/equity) constitutes a hybrid measure, mixing accounting earnings in the numerator with the stock market valuation of assets in the denominator. Union effects on the return to equity should be small, since the rate of return to investors should tend toward equality across investment paths. That is, lower earnings by a union company (shown in the numerator) will decrease that firm's equity value (in the denominator), but generally have small effects on the ratio.

Union effects on firm market value reflect investors' expectations about unionism's impact on the present value of future earnings. Market value measures provide forward-looking, risk-adjusted estimates of union effects. These effects on market value can differ from unionism's impact on current earnings. For example, a union may significantly decrease current earnings but not market value if investors believe the firm can adjust in the future or in some way offset the union's current negative impact. Or, a union may have little immediate impact on earnings but significantly decrease market value if investors expect the union to have a detrimental effect on firm growth and future earnings. Empirical studies examining union effects on market value have typically measured profitability by either Tobin's q (which will be used here), representing market value divided by the replacement cost of assets, or by changes in market value resulting from the "unanticipated" portion of union-related events (e.g., a union representation election).

This study will examine union-nonunion differences in accounting rates of return and market value during the 1970s. A principal advantage of this analysis will be the use of company-specific (rather than industry-specific) data on collective bargaining coverage, which potentially allows us to distinguish the effects of firm coverage, industry coverage, and numerous other firm and industry determinants of profitability. To be examined are overall union effects on alternative profitability measures, changes in these effects over the 1968-1980 period, differences in the magnitude of the union profit effect across broad 2-digit industries, sources from which unions appear to extract gains, variation in the union effect with the extent of firm coverage (i.e., the linearity of the union-profits relationship), and the sensitivity of estimates to specification. One of the principal arguments of this study is that union rent-seeking affects firm investment behavior. Thus, we also will link any evidence of union profit effects to subsequent evidence on investment decisions by the firm.

Union Bargaining Outcomes, Quasi-Rents,
and Investment Behavior

Unions and firms engage in repeated bargaining over what are typically unlimited time horizons. Cooperative bargaining outcomes, if possible, would maximize the sum of the firm's market value, representing the discounted stream of future expected earnings to shareholders, and the present value of expected rents accruing to the union. Cooperative or "efficient" bargaining outcomes could be nondistortionary if labor market conditions were stable, contracts were binding for very long time periods, and the time horizon over which the union evaluates its welfare was at least as long as the life of the firm's prospective new capital. In practice, however, one observes long-run repetitive bargaining governed by short-term (typically three-year) contracts, accompanied by often unpredictable changes in labor and product market conditions. Both parties *may* be deterred from engaging in short-term opportunistic behavior when such behavior is expected to have deleterious effects on future contract negotiations. But even if such cooperative bargaining obtains, union-management bargaining will still distort investment decisions (relative to a nonunion firm) if the union's time horizon is relatively short or, stated similarly, if the union discounts the future at a higher rate than shareholders.[2]

As argued previously, union myopia is likely since the time period over which voting rank-and-file or, more precisely, members with median preferences evaluate their welfare is likely to be shorter than the life of current or prospective firm-specific capital. In particular, influential rank-and-file may have limited time horizons if they have few remaining work years and face little prospect of layoffs owing to reverse seniority provisions. They have little stake in the future financial health of the firm if they cannot sell (or transfer to relatives or friends) their union membership, and if they do not own significant amounts of the company's stock. To the extent that a worker's future pension payments are contingent upon the future health of the company, the worker's time horizon is lengthened, although such a response may be mitigated by government pension guarantees. Thus, cooperative long-run bargaining outcomes between a firm and a myopic union may shift income streams (relative to a nonunion outcome) toward the present by taxing long-lived capital already in place and decreasing current investment in tangible and intangible capital.

While cooperative long-run bargaining outcomes are possible, they are unlikely to systematically prevail over noncooperative outcomes, since both parties have incentive to behave opportunistically. The union is willing to lower its current wage demand in exchange for an employment level greater than that shown on the labor-demand curve, or in the expectation of realizing higher future employment and wages than would otherwise occur. Once a contract is in place, however, the firm has incentive to decrease its use of labor to a point on the labor-demand curve. Firms also can appropriate returns on specific human capital (Klein, Crawford, and Alchian 1978; Crawford 1988). Opportunistic behavior by the firm, however, may be effectively constrained as long as it must renegotiate contracts with the union on a recurring basis and if the union can maintain a credible threat to impose large costs on the firm through means of a strike.[3]

The union typically has greater incentive than the firm to engage in opportunistic or noncooperative behavior inconsistent with long-term *joint* wealth maximization. Once specific assets are brought on line, a union with bargaining power and a credible strike threat is likely to appropriate some portion of the quasi-rents that comprise the normal returns to investment. This situation can be characterized as one of nonbinding contracts in that the length of the labor contract is less than the life of specific capital, so that once the capital is in place, labor can "reopen" bargaining every three or so years. Firms will respond to the union tax on specific capital by reducing investment until the after-tax rate of return equals the market rate of return on investment.[4]

There are few mechanisms by which to move the union and firm from a noncooperative to a cooperative long-term outcome.[5] The union could pledge a future low-wage bargaining strategy in return for the firm's promise to increase investment in specific capital. But in the absence of a bond held by a third party, the union's ability to renege on its promise would prevent such a declaration from being credible (van der Ploeg 1987). The firm might encourage union members to adopt a longer run outlook through increased reliance on compensation in the form of the company's stock and greater back-end loading of the contract (bonuses based on current profits, as opposed to the stock price, are not likely to expand workers' time horizon). But risky and delayed compensation is not likely to appeal to senior rank-and-file. Perhaps the most powerful incentive to extend rank-and-file's time horizon and encourage cooperative union behavior is management's control over pension funds. Indeed, Ippolito (1985; 1988) has argued that unionized companies have incentive to underfund their pension plans in order to moderate future union wage demands.[6]

The union rent-seeking model, therefore, predicts unambiguously a reduction in investment among unionized companies as compared to their nonunion counterparts. Even if union and management engage in cooperative long-run wealth maximization, union myopia will discourage investment in specific long-lived capital. And in the more likely case of noncooperative bargaining outcomes, union bargaining power will be employed to tax the quasi-rents accruing to fixed tangible and intangible capital, further reducing firm investment. Reductions in long-lived capital will subsequently reduce a union's bargaining power and wage demands.

It is worth noting briefly differences between the bargaining model approach to union rent-seeking developed above and the standard microeconomic model of union settlements on-the-demand curve. The standard model treats the union wage as an *exogenous* change in the factor price. In response to an increase in the wage, the profit-maximizing firm decreases employment. The effect on capital usage is indeterminate. On the one hand, the increase in the wage lowers the relative price of capital, leading to an increase in optimal capital usage and investment (a substitution effect). On the other hand, the decrease in profit-maximizing output associated with the union cost increase causes an increase in demand (a scale effect). Thus, the net effect on capital investment resulting from an exogenous wage increase is indeterminate, depending on the size of the relative demand shifts. The standard model does predict, however, that the capital-labor ratio will increase in response to a wage increase.

The on-the-demand curve outcome is not in general Pareto optimal, however, since there exist potential settlements off-the-demand curve preferred by both the union and firm. The potential gain from simultaneous bargaining over wages and employment can be seen in figure 2.1, which shows not only the firm's labor demand curve, but also the union's utility curve, U_i, and the firm's isoprofit curve, π_i, at the on-the-demand curve settlement (w_2, L_2). The lens-shaped area formed by the intersection of these two curves contains wage-employment combinations preferred by both parties. "Efficient" contract settlements lie along a contract curve formed by the tangencies of U_i and π_i. The "strong efficiency" case corresponds to a vertical contract curve, CC, at the competitive employment level, L_1. In this special case, the competitive employment and capital-labor ratio obtain in the short run; i.e., holding constant the level of capital.

The strong efficiency case can be further illustrated by contrasting it with the inefficient on-the-demand curve case. Subject to constraints, let the union maximize "rents,"

(2.1)   max $R = (w_u - w_c)L$,   (union maximand)

where w_u is the realized union wage, w_c is the opportunity cost or competitive wage (we ignore the effect of unions on nonunion wages), and L is employment. R, a measure of the excess of the union wage bill over the competitive wage bill, has been a common maximand assumed in the literature (e.g., Rosen 1969). The firm in turn maximizes profits, π, given w_u. That is,

(2.2)   max $\pi = PQ - rK - w_uL$,   (firm maximand)

where Q is output, P product price, K capital, r the price of capital, and all else as defined above. Sequential wage-employment determination, wherein the union maximizes R and the firm responds by selecting L to maximize profits, given w_u, corresponds to the on-the-demand curve outcome (w_2, L_2) shown in figure 2.1.

An efficient bargaining situation on a vertical contract curve implies that the two parties will maximize the total value of the enterprise V (Abowd 1989b), being the sum of firm profits (π) and union rents (R), and then bargain over division of the surplus. Maximizing V results in the same output, price, and input usage as obtains in the case where the firm maximizes π subject to the competitive wage or opportunity cost wage, w_c; that is,

$$(2.3) \quad \max V = \pi + R$$
$$= PQ - rK - w_uL + (w_u - w_c)L$$
$$= PQ - rK - w_cL.$$

The firm, therefore, adjusts employment according to the opportunity cost wage and not its "own" wage.[7] Here, the union has no *short-run* real effects; rather, $Q, P, K,$ and L are identical to the competitive case. The union or own wage is indeterminate.

Figure 2.1
Short-Run Bargaining Model

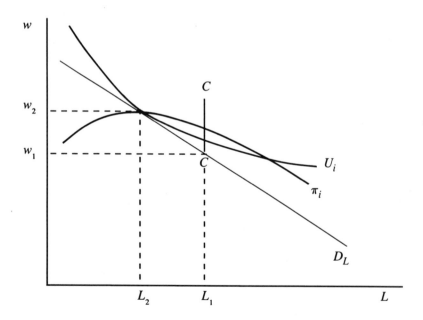

By contrast, the rent-seeking model outlined here is a long-run bargaining model in which capital stocks are assumed to be variable. As discussed previously, the bargaining model treats the wage premium as an *outcome* of union rent-seeking made possible by the existence of monopoly returns and quasi-rents. In the long run, the equivalency between the union and competitive outcomes shown in eq. (2.3) breaks down. First, capital and other fixed-cost inputs are no longer fixed and are free to vary between union and nonunion firms. Moreover, if eq. (2.3) is converted from a single-period model to a multiperiod present value model, the equivalency between the outcomes no longer holds. The reason for this is that the present value of $w_u L$ evaluated by the union does not match the present value of $w_u L$ evaluated by the firm, since the union is evaluating it over a shorter time period (or more highly discounting the future). Thus, the $w_u L$ terms in the second line of eq. (2.3) no longer cancel out.

Our primary interest is to examine the effects of union rent-seeking on the firm's investment activity. As developed previously, it was seen that the rent-seeking model predicts lower investment in long-lived specific tangible and intangible capital than would occur in the absence of the union. In addition to a "direct" union effect on investment, owing to the union tax on returns emanating from tangible and intangible capital, union rent-seeking is likely to have an "indirect" effect on investment (Hirsch, forthcoming). Indirect effects result if unions decrease company earnings, and if such earnings provide a low-cost source of funds for firm investments. Subsequent empirical analysis will attempt to distinguish unionism's direct and indirect effects.

Graphically, union rent-seeking can be represented as levying a tax on the returns associated with relation-specific tangible and intangible capital. Figure 2.2 (a–c) presents diagrams showing curves labeled MRI, representing the marginal rate of return on investment, and MFC, representing the marginal financing cost of funds. Initially, we assume that the firm faces constant marginal financing costs (this would occur in a world with a neutral tax system and a competitive capital market with no transaction/information costs). Firms will carry out investment up to the point where the marginal rate of return on investment equals

Figure 2.2
Union Effects on Investment

(a)

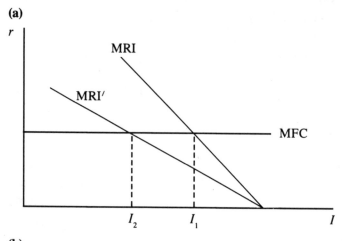

(b)

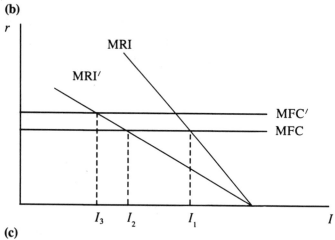

(c)

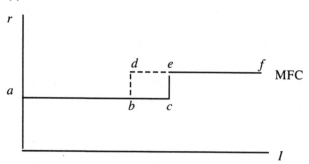

marginal costs, corresponding to investment level I_1 in figure 2.2(a). This framework can be applied not only to investment in physical capital, but also to investment in intangible capital such as R&D.

The union tax on the prospective returns to investment flattens or rotates downward the MRI curve to MRI$'$, with a slope of $(1-t)S$, where S is the absolute value of the slope of the nonunion MRI curve and t is the tax rate (i.e., the proportion of the return to capital appropriated by the union). The union tax places a wedge between nonunion and union rates of return, so the union firm reduces investment until its after-tax rate of return is equal to its marginal financing costs. In figure 2.2(a), this implies a reduction in investment from I_1 to I_2; marginal and average rates of return on investment are lower for a union than for a nonunion firm at any given level of investment. If the MFC schedule were upward sloping, the equilibrium decrease in I would be somewhat smaller owing to the falling opportunity cost of funds at lower levels of I.

The effect of the union tax on investment activity is more complicated if union coverage affects the marginal financing cost. Assume for sake of illustration that the lower profitability owing to union bargaining power causes an upward shift in marginal financing costs, from MFC to MFC$'$, as seen in figure 2.2(b). In this case, investment falls from I_1 to I_3, owing both to the *direct* effect of the union tax from I_1 to I_2, and to an *indirect* effect associated with the higher financing cost from I_2 to I_3. Perhaps a more realistic case is an MFC curve that is discontinuous at the point where a firm must shift from internal to external financing of investment. Figure 2.2(c) identifies such an MFC schedule. In the non-union case, the MFC schedule is represented by *acef*; at point c the firm must shift from internal to external funds. In the union case, retained earnings or profits are reduced, leading to the MFC schedule *abdf*, the upward shift now occurring at the lower level b. In this case, if both the pre- and postunion tax MRI schedules intersect MFC to the right of point e, or to the left of point b, the entire union effect on I will be a direct effect. Intuitively, the union will have no indirect effect if the *marginal* financing cost is unchanged; that is, if the firm would rely on external marginal financing with or without a union, or if it relies entirely on internal funds with or without a union. Otherwise, there will be both a direct and an indirect union effect on investment activity.

Although different from the traditional model, the union rent-seeking approach, which treats union wage demands as endogenous, does not rule out the existence of substitution and scale effects. Union bargaining power facilitates cost increases that unambiguously reduce output (scale) and hence usage of all factor inputs. And if the union tax on capital can be reduced by a reduction in employment, the traditional substitution effect is more likely to operate. Substitution or relative price effects will affect the mix as well as level of investment, leading to relatively lower use of factors taxed heavily by the union, and greater reliance on factors whose returns are difficult for unions to appropriate. For example, unionized firms are likely to decrease investment in long-lived capital with high fixed costs, and in innovative activity that leads to firm-specific returns. By contrast, the firm may increase investment in technologies and innovative activity expected to lead to labor-saving and whose returns are not vulnerable to union appropriation. Note that long-lived, specific physical capital is perhaps most vulnerable to union capture, even if such capital is labor-saving. Of course, the net effect of unions on input use and investments in tangible and intangible capital is ultimately an empirical question.

Union rent-seeking is likely to reduce not only investment in physical capital, but also investment in R&D and other forms of innovative activity. The stock of knowledge and improvements in processes and products emanating from R&D are likely to be relatively long-lived and firm specific. To the extent that the returns from innovative activity are appropriable, firms will respond to union power by reducing these investments. Collective bargaining coverage within a company is most likely to reduce investment in product innovations and relatively factor-neutral process innovations, while having ambiguous effects on labor-saving process innovation.[8] R&D expenditures also tend to signal, or be statistically prior to, investments in physical capital.[9] Therefore, firms reducing long-range plans for physical capital investment in response to union rent-seeking are likely to reduce investment in R&D.

Patents applied for or granted are a measure of innovative *output* emanating from a company's R&D stock. Patent activity is likely to exhibit a relationship with company union coverage largely similar to that exhibited by R&D inputs. Unionized companies, however, may be more likely to patent, given their stock of innovation capital, as a means of reducing union rent appropriation (Connolly, Hirsch, and Hirschey 1986). Although the patent application process is often costly and revealing of trade secrets, patents offer the opportunity for firms to license product and process innovations. The opportunity to license transforms what might otherwise be firm-specific innovative capital into general capital, and lessens a union's ability to appropriate the quasi-rents from that capital.[10]

A final point worth emphasizing is that most collective bargaining agreements are made at the plant (establishment) or multiplant level, rather than for the entire firm. To the extent that capital and production can easily be shifted to nonunion plants within a firm, a union's ability to appropriate returns from investment may be constrained. In fact, a firm's implicit or explicit threat to transfer production to nonunion plants may limit union wage demands. To the extent that unionized operations remain vital to the firm, however, union labor can still appropriate a share of a firm's quasi-rents emanating from capital in its nonunion operations. Similarly, the threat of union organizing in nonunion plants and wage standardization across union and nonunion plants within a firm lessen a firm's ability to avoid the union tax through a reallocation of capital away from its unionized plants. Ultimately, it is an empirical question as to how unionization affects firm performance and investment behavior. Data on within-firm or establishment-level allocations of investment funds and economic performance, however, would enhance our understanding of the process (see Verma 1985).

Summary

Unions and firms engage in a repeated bargaining relationship in which the union attempts to appropriate quasi-rents emanating from firm-specific capital. Rent-seeking by the union results in lower earnings and market value among union companies than among similar nonunion companies. The level and mix of capital investment is affected in turn because of the union tax on the quasi-rents that make up the normal returns to investment and because earnings, which provide a low-cost source of funds, are lower. Union effects on investment behavior will result even if cooperative or jointly maximizing long-run bargaining outcomes obtain, owing to myopia on the part of senior rank-and-file. Union effects on investment will be more negative if non-cooperative bargaining outcomes are the norm. Most likely to be affected by union rent-seeking are investments in long-lived, relation-specific physical capital, and innovative activity leading to firm-specific innovation and subsequent physical capital. Union companies are expected to have a higher propensity to patent, given their R&D stock, as a means of decreasing the union tax on quasi-rents.

The analysis to this point has assumed that unions have no significant effect on productivity in the firm. If unions do have systematic effects on productivity, the above analysis must be qualified since union effects could either reinforce or offset changes in compensation costs engendered by union rent-seeking. Unions will affect productivity and productivity growth indirectly, via their effects on investment behavior and the use of inputs. Less clear is the direct role of unionism in affecting productivity and productivity growth independent of levels and changes in input usage. Union effects on productivity have been the focus of considerable study in recent years, whereas relatively little attention has been given to productivity growth. We turn to these issues in chapter 6.

NOTES

1. To the extent that patents result from previous investments in R&D or other forms of innovative activity, the returns on patents might best be considered a quasi-rent. Of course, notions of fairness in the labor market also may produce a positive relationship between profits and wages, even if resources are relatively mobile. For an example of such a model, see Akerlof (1982).

2. For such a model, see Bronars and Deere (1989) and related discussions in Hirsch (1990a, forthcoming).

3. See Reder and Neumann (1980) for a discussion of bargaining "protocols" that develop between management and labor. A firm (or industry) in failing condition may encourage opportunistic behavior by both management and the union. That is, noncooperative bargaining outcomes become more likely as one moves from infinitely repeated bargaining to a time-limited bargaining horizon. Lawrence and Lawrence (1985) examine the case of a declining industry with large fixed costs in long-lived capital. They argue that labor demand elasticity will decrease since substituting capital for labor is less attractive in a declining industry. Hence, union bargaining

power and the wage premium may *increase* in the short run. Over the long run, employment and output will be substantially reduced. They believe their model applies with some force to the U.S. steel industry.

4. See Grout (1984) for an examination of investment decisions in situations with binding and nonbinding contracts. Baldwin (1983) contends that firms will respond to union "expropriation" of returns by retaining second-best or relatively less productive capital as a means of moderating union wage demands. Union wage demands commensurate with productivity at a firm's efficient plants would then necessitate shutdowns at the firm's less efficient plants. Tauman and Weiss (1987) develop a duopoly model in which union and nonunion firms select their technologies.

5. Baldwin (1983) explores several possibilities. Wachter and Cohen (1988) propose a cooperative implicit contract rule (named the "sunk-cost loss rule") wherein firms faced with declining demand can lower their wage bill through a reduction in hours but not wages, thus insuring that profits are reduced.

6. Interestingly, government regulations and guarantees with respect to pension funding, although defensible on other grounds, lessen union members' stake in the long-run future of the firm and their union. A similar argument can be made with respect to antidiscrimination (nepotism) laws applied to unions if, in their absence, rank-and-file could pass on membership to friends and relatives.

7. The prediction that a union firm will adjust employment to the labor market or opportunity cost wage, and not to its own wage, has formed the basis for some of the empirical tests of strong efficiency. Among the papers in this area are Brown and Ashenfelter (1986), McCurdy and Pencavel (1986), Card (1986), Eberts and Stone (1986), and Svejnar (1986).

8. Most company-financed R&D is described as product R&D, although many final products in the producer goods sector end up as inputs into the production process of firms downstream.

9. Lach and Schankerman (1989) provide evidence that R&D "Granger causes" capital investment, but investment doesn't Granger cause R&D.

10. We treat the ratio of patents to R&D stock as a measure of patent propensity, and expect unionized companies to have higher ratios. Alternatively, the ratio can be considered a measure of R&D efficiency—firms with higher ratios achieve greater innovative output from given inputs. By this interpretation, union companies also should have higher patent to R&D stock ratios since the union tax on investment returns implies a higher before-tax rate of return (or productivity) to innovative activity in union companies. Empirical analyses of R&D and patents are found in Griliches (1984). Levin et al. (1987) discuss numerous factors determining the appropriability of returns from R&D, but do not mention labor unions.

3
Union Coverage Among U.S. Firms

Union Coverage Survey

In this study, the relationship between union coverage and various dimensions of economic performance are examined at the firm level. A serious limitation of past studies has been the difficulty in measuring union coverage at the level of the firm.[1] There are no publicly available data on the extent of union coverage among U.S. companies. The Bureau of Labor Statistics (BLS) does collect and publish announcements of union contract agreements covering large groups of workers. Firm-level coverage figures can thus be constructed by aggregating the number of covered workers across all of a firm's listed contracts and dividing that sum by total employees in a firm. Such calculations are neither simple nor necessarily reliable. Beyond the nontrivial problem of matching individual contract information to the appropriate firm(s), there is no mandatory reporting of contract information. Hence, estimates of the proportion of a firm's workforce covered by a collective bargaining agreement will understate actual union coverage, since only large contracts are included, and since there may be incomplete recording of these contracts.[2]

The difficulty in obtaining firm-level information on union coverage has prompted authors of previous firm-level studies examining union effects on economic performance (Salinger 1984; Connolly, Hirsch, and Hirschey 1986; Hirsch and Connolly 1987; Bronars and Deere 1989) to match 3-digit industry-level data, based on calculations from the May Current Population Surveys, to individual firms. Such studies, however, fail to account for what may be considerable intraindustry variation in unionization, and entangle to an unknown degree union and industry effects on market value, investments in tangible and intangible capital, and productivity.

As part of this study, a survey of U.S. firms was conducted in order to obtain more direct and reliable information on union coverage. The survey, conducted during late 1987 and 1988, contacted firms from a master list of 1,904 firms taken from the *R&D Master File*, a data file comprised of all publicly traded manufacturing sector companies operating in 1976 that were included on *Compustat* tapes during 1976-1978.[3] Firms were asked to answer the following question for 1987 and, as best they could, for 1977 (as their company then existed):

> To the best of your knowledge, approximately what percentage of your corporation's total North American workforce is covered by collective bargaining agreements?

The largest 300 firms (based on 1976 sales) were contacted by phone and/or mail and received a follow-up questionnaire if they did not initially respond; the remaining firms were mailed a questionnaire.[4] Union data for 1977 corresponds to the firm *as it existed* in 1977. In cases where firms had merged, efforts were made to acquire union figures for the operating units as they existed in 1977.

Usable data for 1977 or 1987 were obtained from 475 firms through the mail and phone survey. A direct measure of 1977 union coverage was obtained from 460 firms; 467 firms provided 1987 figures; and 452 firms provided both 1977 and 1987 figures. The relatively few firms not providing 1977 data typically indicated the data were not available and they could not provide an estimate. Firms for which 1977 but not 1987 data were available were those that were publicly traded in 1977, but are now a subsidiary or fully integrated part of a merged firm.

The empirical work in this monograph utilizes a constructed measure of 1977 union coverage, available for a total of 632 firms. In addition to the 460 firms for which a direct measure of 1977 coverage was obtained, we estimate 1977 coverage for an additional 15 firms based on reported 1987 coverage figures in the same survey, and for 157 firms based on firm coverage figures collected in an independent 1972 Conference Board Survey (see below). Union coverage figures for 1977 were estimated for the 15 firms by multiplying the 1987 figures by 1.22, based on the ratio of 1977- to-1987 coverage data among the 452 firms for which both years of data were available (the simple correlation between the 1977 and 1987 figures is 0.87).

The 1972 union data were kindly provided by David C. Hershfield, who developed the figures from data collected in a 1972 survey by the Conference Board. These data, measuring the percentage of production and maintenance workers covered by a collective bargaining agreement, were available for 315 Fortune 1000 firms in our data base, 157 for which we could not obtain a response in our survey, and 158 for which we obtained 1977 data (data from the merged surveys for 1972, 1977, and 1987 were available for 154 firms). Because we are interested in the extent of unionization within the entire firm, the 1972 coverage figures for production workers were multiplied by the estimated proportion of production workers in the firm based on 2-, 3-, and 4-digit SIC industry figures for 1972. This conversion assumes zero coverage among nonproduction workers, thus biasing downward the total firm coverage estimates. Data for 1972 *and* 1977 were available for 158 firms; total workforce coverage figures were about 20 percent higher in 1972 than in 1977 among these firms (the two measures had a simple correlation of 0.71). The 157 firms for whom only 1972 data were available were assigned a 1977 coverage estimate equal to 0.84 times the adjusted 1972 figure.

We do not believe the empirical results or conclusions presented in subsequent chapters are affected substantially by response bias in the survey. The *R&D Master File* included information on virtually all firms in the target population—publicly traded firms in the manufacturing sector. From this population, the union survey sample contains a disproportionate number of large companies. But the number of small companies who responded to the survey is substantial and firm size is a control variable in subsequent empirical work. As a check for possible survey bias, measures of profitability and investment were compared among companies for whom firm union coverage is measured and companies in the *R&D Master File* for whom no union measure is available. Differences in these measures between responding and nonresponding companies are small, and never close to statistical significance once firm size and industry group are controlled.

The determination of firms' union status is not a principal focus of this monograph. Firm-level union coverage information, however, is interesting in its own right, particularly so since such figures are not widely available. In tables 3.1 and 3.2, union coverage figures for 1972, 1977, and 1987, disaggregated by industry category, are presented. Data for three samples of firms are included: the 154 companies for whom 1972, 1977, and 1987 union coverage figures are available (table 3.1); the 452 companies for whom data were obtained in this survey for both 1977 and 1987 (table 3.2); and the 632 firms for whom 1977 union coverage was directly obtained, or estimated based on data from 1972 or 1987 (table 3.2). This latter measure, designated by UN, is the union coverage measure utilized in the monograph's subsequent chapters.[5]

The secular decline in union coverage among U.S. firms is evident from the data presented in both tables. Table 3.1 presents coverage figures for the 154 Fortune 1000 firms for whom coverage data were available from the 1972 Conference Board Survey, and for both 1977 and 1987 from the 1987 Hirsch survey conducted for this project. While intertemporal changes are not measured precisely due to differences in the periods and the nature of the surveys, the magnitude of the changes in sample means is large. Union coverage among these relatively large companies is estimated to have declined from 41.6 percent in 1972, to 34.9 percent in 1977, and to 28.3 percent in 1987. A comparable trend over the last decade is evident for the 452 firms in the Hirsch survey (table 3.2, columns (2) and (3)): coverage declines from 30.5 percent in 1977 to 25.0 percent in 1987. In fact, union coverage declined in 19 out of the 20 industry categories, the exception being electrical equipment and supplies, where coverage remained roughly constant at a low level of about 7 percent. Union coverage is lower among firms in this larger sample than in the 154-firm sample because the Hirsch survey included firms outside the Fortune 1000, among whom zero union coverage was not uncommon.

The reliability of the estimated intertemporal change in union coverage cannot be known with certainty. Differences between the 1972 and 1977 figures arise not only because of changes in coverage over time, but also because the data are derived from different surveys, the 1977 figures were reported in 1987, and the 1972 figures were converted from a measure of coverage among production workers to a measure of coverage among total workers. The 1977 and 1987 figures are more comparable in that they derive from the same survey and responses were provided

Table 3.1
Company Union Coverage Figures by Industry: 1972, 1977, and 1987

	n	COV-72 mean	COV-72 s.d.	COV-77 mean	COV-77 s.d.	COV-87 mean	COV-87 s.d.
Total	154	41.6	(27.6)	34.9	(24.9)	28.3	(23.8)
Food & kindred products	12	45.1	(19.9)	45.7	(22.0)	39.2	(20.1)
Textiles & apparel	6	11.8	(25.9)	5.3	(9.1)	4.4	(9.6)
Chemicals, excluding drugs	18	41.0	(15.1)	30.6	(16.4)	21.7	(13.4)
Drugs & medical instruments	8	9.1	(13.3)	12.7	(13.9)	10.1	(10.6)
Petroleum refining	12	32.0	(19.3)	18.5	(9.9)	11.6	(8.1)
Rubber & miscellaneous plastics	4	50.1	(18.4)	33.8	(17.4)	30.2	(20.2)
Stone, clay, & glass	5	43.4	(35.6)	25.9	(22.5)	16.7	(15.4)
Primary metals	10	72.6	(18.0)	67.6	(18.8)	63.2	(23.2)
Fabricated metal products	3	58.1	(26.7)	41.0	(29.5)	33.7	(27.4)
Engines, farm & const. equip.	10	61.9	(10.7)	42.0	(15.6)	31.1	(15.7)
Office, computers, & acct. equip.	7	8.0	(10.0)	8.2	(9.7)	5.2	(8.0)
Other machinery, not electric	7	27.2	(20.1)	26.1	(18.9)	21.6	(25.6)
Electrical equipment & supplies	6	29.7	(33.1)	20.6	(24.8)	16.3	(22.0)
Communication equipment	9	60.3	(15.6)	54.9	(16.0)	36.5	(21.2)
Motor vehicle and transp. equip.	13	63.2	(26.3)	51.4	(21.7)	47.5	(26.7)
Aircraft & aerospace	3	12.8	(14.3)	32.5	(33.5)	20.2	(16.4)
Professional & scientific equip.	5	20.6	(28.3)	29.0	(39.7)	23.0	(32.7)
Lumber, wood, & paper	7	47.9	(30.9)	46.4	(31.6)	45.9	(21.2)
Misc. manuf. & conglomerates	9	44.3	(26.4)	37.5	(20.7)	30.5	(17.2)

NOTE: The sample is comprised of 154 companies responding in both the Hirsch survey for 1977 and 1987, and the Conference Board Survey for 1972. The surveys are described in the text.

Table 3.2
Company Union Coverage Figures by Industry: 1977 and 1987

	n	UN (1977) (1) mean	s.d.	COV-77 (2) n	mean	s.d.	COV-87 (3) mean	s.d.
Total	632	32.7	(27.3)	452	30.5	(27.8)	25.0	(25.3)
Food & kindred products	60	42.0	(26.6)	39	44.8	(29.2)	40.1	(27.9)
Textiles & apparel	31	24.2	(28.5)	19	18.9	(27.7)	15.5	(22.8)
Chemicals, excluding drugs	37	27.9	(18.3)	30	29.7	(18.6)	23.0	(17.4)
Drugs & medical instruments	34	15.6	(18.4)	27	16.5	(19.6)	10.4	(15.6)
Petroleum refining	27	29.8	(18.2)	25	29.7	(18.3)	21.9	(17.0)
Rubber & miscellaneous plastics	24	37.0	(24.9)	14	32.4	(26.8)	27.9	(26.8)
Stone, clay, & glass	24	45.1	(24.0)	17	41.6	(27.3)	35.5	(26.5)
Primary metals	40	61.5	(20.0)	20	67.7	(19.7)	62.1	(23.2)
Fabricated metal products	33	31.9	(28.9)	23	27.3	(30.4)	20.7	(22.1)
Engines, farm & const. equip.	26	36.0	(21.5)	21	31.3	(21.3)	23.0	(17.8)
Office, computers, & acct. equip.	21	4.4	(7.4)	18	4.7	(7.9)	2.4	(5.6)
Other machinery, not electric	43	34.9	(26.7)	30	29.5	(26.6)	21.1	(23.0)
Electrical equipment & supplies	43	8.5	(16.7)	38	6.9	(15.5)	7.0	(16.2)
Communication equipment	26	43.9	(23.7)	18	43.8	(22.5)	32.6	(20.7)
Motor vehicle and transp. equip.	39	48.9	(25.3)	28	47.0	(27.1)	38.0	(26.1)
Aircraft & aerospace	11	27.2	(23.0)	9	31.0	(23.9)	18.4	(19.0)
Professional & scientific equip.	28	10.8	(22.1)	21	11.4	(23.9)	10.7	(21.2)
Lumber, wood, & paper	44	36.6	(29.8)	30	36.0	(29.6)	33.2	(26.5)
Misc. manuf. & conglomerates	41	33.2	(25.1)	25	34.2	(26.1)	30.3	(25.6)

NOTE: Columns reporting COV-77 and COV-87 are for the sample of 452 companies reporting both 1977 and 1987 union coverage in the Hirsch survey. UN represents estimated union coverage in 1977 for 632 firms providing information in either the Hirsch or Conference Board surveys. Construction of UN is described in the text.

by the same person for both years. Many firms, however, did not have records of 1977 union coverage, and the reliability of the respondents' estimates for 1977 cannot be directly ascertained.

Confidence in the reported union coverage figures is enhanced by comparison with other available figures. Mean union coverage in 1977 for the full 632-firm sample is estimated to be 32.7 percent. For the 452-firm Hirsch survey sample, the corresponding figure is 30.5 percent, while for the smaller 154-firm sample for which data from both surveys are available, union coverage is estimated to be 34.9 percent. These figures can be compared to the figure of 36.8 percent coverage among *eligible* workers in all manufacturing, based on union membership data from the 1976-1978 May Current Population Surveys (Kokkelenberg and Sockell 1985, table 4). Calculated union density among *all* would be about 2 percentage points lower, or 35 percent (see Curme, Hirsch, and Macpherson 1990, p. 9). Estimated 1987 union coverage among the 452 firms in the Hirsch survey is 25.0 percent. This is very close to the 25.8 percent figure reported by CPA firm Grant Thornton in a 1987 survey of manufacturing firms (*Wall Street Journal*, 5-31-88, p. 1), and the 24.7 percent coverage figure among manufacturing employees derived from the 1987 CPS household surveys (U.S. Bureau of the Census 1989, table 684).

Interindustry and intraindustry variation in firm-level union coverage is substantial. Tables 3.1 and 3.2 provide means and standard deviations of coverage by 2-digit manufacturing industry; we focus on table 3.2, where sample sizes within industry categories are largest.[6] Dispersion of firm union coverage is large within most broad industry categories. In fact, in 1987 there was at least one firm in every industry category with zero union coverage (there were two industry categories with no nonunion companies in 1977). The substantial intraindustry variation in unionization supports the proposition that measurement of union coverage at the firm level is essential for obtaining reliable estimates of union effects on firm performance.

The least highly organized industry categories are office, computers, and accounting equipment; electrical equipment and supplies; professional and scientific equipment; and drugs and medical instruments. Although union coverage among firms in these industries is relatively low and declining, unionization among firms in most industries remains substantial. Average coverage among all firms in 1987 was 25.0 percent; coverage figures among production workers only are substantially higher.[7] Unionization remains widely prevalent among firms in the primary metals (62.1 percent), food and kindred products (40.1 percent), and motor vehicle and transportation equipment (38.0 percent) industries. Declines in firm union coverage between 1977 and 1987 were particularly large in the aircraft and aerospace, communication equipment, motor vehicle and transportation equipment, and engines, farm, and construction equipment industries.

Based on these data, it is tempting to draw inferences regarding causes of union decline over this period. We make no such attempt at this point. The results of the firm-level surveys on union coverage, summarized in tables 3.1 and 3.2, do illustrate two points, however. First, substantial intraindustry variation in union coverage make it essential to use firm-level coverage measures in econometric analyses of union effects. Second, the large differences in average unionization across industry categories makes it necessary to carefully control for a broad array of industry measures in estimating union effects on firm performance.[8]

Construction of the Data Set

Empirical analysis in this monograph matches the firm-level union survey information discussed previously with firm- and industry-specific financial, investment, and production data. The *R&D Master File*, comprised of publicly traded manufacturing sector companies operating in 1976, was constructed at the National Bureau of Economic Research and Harvard University and matches company data from *Compustat* with U.S. patents data from the Office of Technology Assessment and Forecasting.[9] *Compustat*, which is produced by Standard & Poor's (S&P) Compustat Services, Inc., provides computer-readable "libraries" of financial, statistical, and market information covering several thousand industrial and nonindustrial companies. Information is obtained from 10-K reports filed with the Securities and Exchange Commission, company reports to shareholders, other S&P publications, telephone contacts, and stock market information services. The *R&D Master File* utilizes information from various industrial *Compustat* files.

The *R&D Master File* provides panel data for companies for the years 1958 through 1980. Because missing data increase as one moves away from 1976 and no time-series union coverage is available, subsequent analysis focuses on the years 1968-1980. The data file contains relatively complete reporting of company market value, accounting rates of return, gross and net plant, and the book value of debt; less complete reporting of R&D investment and patents; and relatively incomplete reporting of advertising expenditures and labor compensation.

Industry data on shipments, capital intensity, payroll, and the ratio of production to total employees are obtained from the Bureau of Industrial Economics tape consolidating data from the Annual Survey of Manufactures. Data on industry concentration (adjusted for imports and regional concentration), as well as import penetration, were available for 1972 and 1977 in data assembled by Weiss and Pascoe (1986). Industry data are matched to the firm at the 2-, 3-, or 4-digit levels, based on the *Compustat* SIC-code variable designating the firm's principal industry in 1976.

Data Appendix 1 presents means and standard deviations for several variables of interest from the data set, cross-tabulated by union status. The data are presented separately for the full sample of 632 firms over the 13-year period 1968-1980, and for firms divided into similarly sized groups of nonunion (UN = 0), "low" coverage (0 < UN < .30), "medium" coverage (.30 ≤ UN < .60), and "high" coverage (UN ≥ .60) companies. Total sample sizes given are significantly less than 13 times 632 owing to missing data. The substantial differences in firm-level and industry-level performance between union and nonunion companies evinced by the variable means make detailed empirical analysis of union impacts on performance essential. Subsequent chapters examine in detail the relationship of company-level union coverage with profitability, market value, investment behavior, productivity, and productivity growth during the 1970s.

NOTES

1. Notable exceptions are Clark (1984), who uses the PIMS Database on lines of business, and single-industry studies of the cement (Clark 1980a; 1980b) and construction (Allen 1986; 1987) industries. Citations to more recent studies are in Addison and Hirsch (1989), Hirsch (1991), and elsewhere in the text.

2. The BLS currently collects information on contracts covering a thousand or more workers; prior to 1981, information was collected for contracts covering 500 or more workers. The Bureau of National Affairs (BNA) collects similar data, including smaller contracts, although these data are proprietary (but see Abowd 1989b). The name of the business on the contract must be matched to the firm name of the parent company, however, since there are no firm-level identifier codes attached to the contract information. Moreover, multiemployer contracts do not provide information on covered workers by firm.

3. The *R&D Master File* is described later in the chapter.

4. Coverage data were collected for additional firms following completion of the empirical work and initial draft of this manuscript. These data are utilized in subsequent research (Hirsch 1991, forthcoming).

5. Subsequent empirical analysis in chapters 4-6 rely on the largest possible samples of firms. When samples are restricted only to those firms for whom a direct 1977 union coverage response is provided in the Hirsch survey, most results are highly similar to those shown.

6. The industry categories, previously utilized in the *R&D Master File*, are taken from Body and Jaffe (no date). Although highly similar, they do not correspond exactly to a 2-digit SIC classification.

7. The survey conducted for this monograph also asked for the percentage of a company's production workforce covered by collective bargaining agreements. Responses to this question were less complete and reliable than responses to the coverage question applying to a company's entire workforce.

8. Subsequent analysis bears out these points. When only an industry measure of union coverage is included in regression models, its coefficient is highly sensitive to specification. When detailed industry control variables are included, its coefficient is close to zero. When few industries are included, their coefficient is often quite large (in absolute value). Because firms are matched only to their primary industry and the industry codes from the *Compustat* and the CPS cannot be matched precisely, there exists far greater measurement error in the industry than in the firm union coverage measure.

9. Documentation on the *R&D Master File* is provided in Cummins et al. (1985) and Body and Jaffe (no date). The data were kindly made available by Zvi Griliches.

4
Labor Unions and Firm Profitability

Union compensation gains can be expected to lower firm profitability, unless they are offset by productivity enhancements in the workplace or higher prices in the product market. Lower profitability will be reflected in decreased current earnings and measured rates of return on capital, and in a lower market valuation of the firm's assets, thus decreasing Tobin's q (market value divided by the replacement cost of physical capital) and other market valuation measures.

Profit-maximizing responses by firms to cost differentials should limit the magnitude of differences in profitability between union and nonunion companies in the very long run. Profit differentials will be reduced through the movement of resources out of union into nonunion sectors. That is, investment in and by union operations will decrease until post-tax (i.e., post-union) rates of return are equivalent to nonunion rates of return or, stated alternatively, union coverage will be restricted to economic sectors realizing above-normal pre-union rates of return. Because the quasi-rents accruing to long-lived capital may provide a principal source for union gains and complete long-run adjustments occur slowly, we are likely to observe differences in profitability at any point in time.[1]

This chapter briefly reviews previous studies examining union effects on profitability. The data set assembled for this study is then employed to examine union-nonunion differences in profitability. In addition to estimating the overall differential, we examine differences in union effects across industries and over time, and explore the possible sources from which unions capture profits. Conclusions and interpretation of the results follow.

Previous empirical analyses find unionization (or unanticipated union contract gains) to be associated with significantly lower profitability, although studies differ in their conclusions regarding the magnitude and source of union gains.[2] Studies using aggregate industry data (e.g.,

35

Freeman 1983; Karier 1985; Voos and Mishel 1986; and Domowitz, Hubbard, and Petersen 1986) typically employ as their dependent variable the industry price-cost margin, PCM, defined by [(Total Revenue - Variable Costs) / Total Revenue] and typically measured by [(Value Added - Payroll - Advertising) / Shipments]. Line of business and some firm-level studies have used accounting profit rate measures: the rate of return on sales, π_s, measured by earnings divided by sales, and the rate of return on capital, π_k, measured by earnings divided by the value of the capital stock (e.g., Clark 1984; Hirsch and Connolly 1987; Hirsch 1990b).

Firm-level analyses of publicly traded firms (e.g., Salinger 1984; Connolly, Hirsch, and Hirschey 1986; Hirsch and Connolly 1987; Hirsch 1990b) have used market value measures of profitability, a common measure being Tobin's q, defined as firm market value divided by the replacement cost of assets. Finally, there have been several "event" studies in which changes in market value attributable to union representation elections or unanticipated changes in collective bargaining agreements have been examined (e.g., Ruback and Zimmerman 1984; Bronars and Deere 1990; Becker 1987; and Abowd 1989b).[3]

The conclusion that unionization is associated with lower profitability holds for studies using industries, firms, or lines of business as the unit of observation; for models where the profitability measures are industry price-cost margins, firm rates of return to capital or sales, Tobin's q or other market value measures, or stock market value changes in response to union "events"; for simultaneous equation as well as single equation models; and regardless of the time period under study.

Despite the consensus that profitability is lower in unionized settings, there is disagreement as to the magnitude of the profit reduction and the sources from which union gains obtain. Economists are understandably skeptical that large profit differentials can survive in a competitive economy, notwithstanding the sizable union-nonunion profit differences found in the empirical literature, and possible econometric biases causing union effects to be understated. There are several potential biases that work to bias toward zero the estimated union effect. First, profit functions are estimated only for *surviving* firms since those for whom union effects are most deleterious may be less likely to remain in the sample.

Second, unions are more likely to be organized where potential profits are higher; hence, the negative union effect on profits may be underestimated in empirical work where union density is treated as exogenous (see Voos and Mishel 1986). Finally, in firm-level studies using an industry-level union density variable, measurement error is likely to bias the union coefficient toward zero. On the other hand, the magnitude of the estimated union-nonunion profit differential is often sensitive to specification. Omission of factors positively correlated with union coverage and negatively correlated with profitability will bias the union profit estimate in the opposite direction

Less attention has been given to the sources from which unions appropriate rents (see Addison and Hirsch 1989). Several studies conclude that unions reduce profits primarily in highly concentrated industries, and that monopoly power provides the primary source for union compensation gains (e.g., Freeman 1983; Salinger 1984; Karier 1985), whereas Clark (1984) finds that unions reduce profits only among businesses with *low* market shares. Hirsch and Connolly (1987) seriously question both sets of findings. They find neither product nor labor market evidence to support the hypothesis that profits associated with industry concentration provide a source for union rents (see also Domowitz, Hubbard, and Petersen 1986). Rather, they argue that returns from firm-specific market shares, R&D capital, and weak foreign competition are more likely sources for union gains. Hirsch (1990b), using a data set with a firm-specific union coverage measure, even more clearly rejects the hypothesis that concentration-related profits provide a source for union rents.

Union Effects on Profitability: Specification and Full-Sample Results

In this chapter, both accounting and market value measures of profitability are examined. Accounting profit rates, measuring realized annual earnings relative to a sales or asset base, are historical and readily available from financial reports. By contrast, market value measures are forward-looking, reflect expected performance over time rather than accounting performance for a single period, measure risk-adjusted returns, and are less likely to be affected by differences in accounting procedures across firms.

Prior to presentation of regression model results, differences in firm-level profit measures, cross-tabulated by union status, warrant mention. Data Appendix 1 presents means of Tobin's q and the rate of return on capital, π_k, for the full sample of firms over the 13-year period 1968-1980, and for firms divided into similar-sized groups of non-union (UN $=$ 0), low-coverage ($0 <$ UN $< .30$), medium-coverage ($.30 \leq$ UN $< .60$), and high-coverage (UN $\geq .60$) companies. Market valuation of firm assets, as measured by Tobin's q, drops sharply with respect to union coverage, particularly as one moves from the non-union to low-union sample of companies (mean q equals 2.34, 1.41, 0.99, and 0.88 for the four union categories, respectively). The suggestion is that even a low level of coverage significantly reduces investors' expectations of future earnings. Likewise, the rate of return on capital, π_k, decreases continuously with respect to union coverage. And in results not presented, gross rates of return on equity, π_e, defined as gross cash flows divided by equity value, do not vary systematically with union coverage (π_e is 0.18, 0.22, 0.20, and 0.21 in the nonunion through high-union categories, respectively). This is to be expected since equity values adjust to differences in expected earnings; that is, if union firms have lower earnings, equity value falls until π_e is similar for union and nonunion firms.[4]

Profitability equations using the natural logarithm of Tobin's q and the rate of return on capital as dependent variables are estimated. A general form of the profit function is:

(4.1) $\pi_{it} = \Sigma \beta_k X_{kit} + \Sigma \psi_j \text{UN} \bullet Z_{jit} + e_{it}$,

where π_{it} is the profitability of firm i in year t, measured alternatively by log(q) and π_k; X includes k firm- and industry-specific variables (including the constant one) that affect profitability directly; β_k are the coefficients attaching to X; and e_{it} is a random error term assumed (for now) to have zero mean and constant variance. Z is a subset of X and includes j firm- and industry-specific variables (including the constant one) that affect profitability in conjunction with unionization of the firm, UN, while ψ_j are the coefficients attaching to UN $\bullet Z$.[5]

Company profits arise from differences between revenues and costs; thus, measurable firm and industry characteristics that affect either revenues or costs may have an impact on profitability. In a competitive market, *economic* profits will tend toward zero in the long run, while large interfirm differences in risk-adjusted profitability at any point in time may signal disequilibrium. Therefore, some portion of the variation in profitability will be associated with differences in firm- and industry-specific sales growth rates, which proxy, in part, disequilibrium-related profits. Because profitability measures reflect accounting as well as economic profits, measured profitability also will differ with respect to company stocks of physical capital, innovative capital (proxied by the R&D stock), and other forms of intangible capital (good will, location, etc.). That is, much of what is measured as profits reflects the normal return to investment and special factors of production.

Market structure may influence price, revenues, and the profitability of firms. Therefore, variables proxying the degree of competition (e.g., industry concentration and import penetration) are included in profit equations. No direct measure of firms' market shares is available for firms in the sample (but see Hirsch 1990b). Union effects on profitability may also differ with respect to market structure; therefore, interaction terms between union coverage and market structure variables warrant examination. Empirical analyses must control as well for size differences among firms, since size may have an impact on costs, or reflect realized efficiencies in the marketplace. Likewise, a union's bargaining power and ability to capture rents may differ systematically with firm size.

The effects of union coverage on profitability should be reflected primarily in the form of union-nonunion differences in wage rates. In subsequent empirical work, we do not directly measure differences in labor costs facing firms but, rather, include a union coverage variable to reflect these cost differences.[6] In the absence of firm-level union coverage or the threat of union organizing, quality-adjusted wage rates should be similar across firms, although there will be real differences owing to differences across areas in labor market conditions, cost of living, taxes, and the like. Stronger support can be furnished for the contention that companies face similar capital prices at any point in time, since new capital and investment funds are relatively mobile. Because factor price differences are not readily measurable, they are not included directly in our profitability equations.

The inclusion of firm and industry union coverage variables is expected to capture important differences in labor costs and the threat of union organizing, respectively. Year dummies capture factor price differences uniformly impacting all firms over time, while industry dummies capture differences uniformly affecting all firms in a broadly defined industry group. Estimated union coefficients will be biased due to the omission of factor prices only to the extent that factor price differences not resulting from union coverage differences are in fact correlated with the error term in the profit equation. The existence or direction of such bias cannot be determined *a priori*.

Initially, a simple specification of eq. (4.1), including only a constant in Z, is estimated. That is, firm unionization, UN, is included in eq. (4.1) as a separate variable, and not in interaction with variables in Z. Among the variables to be included in X are measures of firm size, capital intensity, the R&D stock, firm sales growth, industry concentration, foreign competition, industry sales growth, and dummies for industry and year. Specific variables will be described as empirical results are discussed. Data Appendix 2 provides definitions for all variables used in the profitability regressions.

Unionization is measured in 1977 both at the firm (UN) and industry (I-UN) levels, and is assumed fixed over the period. To be examined subsequently are interactions of UN with variables in Z, interindustry differences in union profit effects, changes over time in unionism's effects, models accounting for varying levels of industry controls, and models correcting for serial correlation of error terms within firms across years. Two important possibilities—omitted variable bias associated with firm fixed effects and simultaneity bias between unionization and profitability—are examined subsequently in a less satisfactory manner.

Initial time-series/cross-section regression results using the entire 1968-1980 panel, with the log of Tobin's q and the rate of return on capital (π_k) as dependent variables, are presented in table 4.1. Complete data are available for 572 firms in 1976, with a smaller number

Table 4.1
Profitability Regression Results

Variable	Dependent variable – log(q)				Dependent variable – π_k			
	(1)	(2)	(3)	(4)	(1')	(2')	(3')	(4')
UN	-0.626 (15.06)	-0.509 (12.88)	-0.555 (17.13)	-0.493 (15.87)	-0.034 (11.90)	-0.027 (9.53)	-0.035 (14.98)	-0.033 (13.74)
R&D-STK/S	0.676 (7.97)	0.182 (2.12)	--	--	-0.009 (1.61)	-0.031 (4.95)	--	--
R&D-STK/S^{est}	--	--	0.707 (9.47)	0.185 (2.22)	--	--	-0.015 (2.74)	-0.034 (5.34)
log(L)	0.019 (2.98)	0.031 (5.15)	0.015 (3.02)	0.023 (4.68)	-0.001 (1.73)	-0.000 (0.36)	-0.001 (2.70)	-0.000 (1.32)
log (K/L)	-0.035 (2.36)	0.010 (0.53)	-0.054 (4.79)	-0.058 (3.87)	-0.003 (2.80)	-0.003 (2.17)	-0.005 (5.89)	-0.008 (7.32)
GROWTH	0.032 (1.05)	0.049 (1.80)	0.008 (0.42)	0.008 (0.45)	0.009 (4.34)	0.009 (4.72)	0.006 (4.63)	0.006 (4.61)
I-GROWTH	1.598 (8.50)	0.844 (4.71)	1.867 (12.19)	1.301 (8.74)	0.102 (7.89)	0.065 (5.03)	0.128 (11.41)	0.103 (9.08)
I-CR4	0.423 (7.06)	0.064 (0.95)	0.563 (12.16)	0.380 (7.09)	0.021 (5.05)	0.004 (0.90)	0.029 (8.62)	0.021 (5.11)
I-DOMSH	0.376 (2.45)	0.087 (0.56)	0.283 (2.25)	0.058 (0.44)	0.011 (1.03)	-0.003 (0.30)	0.012 (1.31)	-0.003 (0.34)

Table 4.1 (continued)

Variable	Dependent variable – log(q)				Dependent variable – π_k			
	(1)	(2)	(3)	(4)	(1')	(2')	(3')	(4')
I-UN	-0.428	-0.012	-0.497	-0.176	-0.006	0.031	-0.008	0.014
	(5.95)	(0.11)	(9.03)	(2.15)	(1.22)	(4.11)	(2.02)	(2.16)
IND	no	yes	no	yes	no	yes	no	yes
YEAR	yes	yes	yes	yes	yes	yes	yes	yes
$\bar{R}^2$	0.332	0.468	0.382	0.480	0.132	0.225	0.149	0.217
n	4,257	4,257	6,248	6,248	4,248	4,248	6,236	6,236

NOTES: $|t|$ in parentheses. Below are coefficients ($|t|$) obtained substituting union dummies for UN in equations (4) and (4'), with nonunion the omitted reference group and where UN-LOW = 1 if ($0 <$ UN $\leq .30$); UN-MED = 1 if ($.30 \leq$ UN $< .60$); and UN-HIGH = 1 if (UN $\geq .60$).

(4): -0.217 UN-LOW – 0.396 UN-MED – 0.371 UN-HIGH.
        (9.68)   (16.92)   (14.85)

(4'): -0.015 UN-LOW – 0.028 UN-MED – 0.026 UN-HIGH.
        (9.01)   (15.52)   (13.65)

of observations in earlier and later years. Total sample sizes are 6,248 for the log(q) equations and 6,236 for the π_k equations. Attention is focused on the coefficients on the time-invariant variable (UN) measuring the proportion of workers covered by a collective bargaining contract in the firm in 1977. In regression results not presented, the estimated effects of unionization on a profitability variable measuring the rate of return to sales are found to be generally similar to those found for π_k.

Regression results presented in table 4.1 include specifications with and without 2-digit industry dummies and for two samples of firms (see below). Coefficients and t-ratios are presented in a table note for a specification omitting UN, but instead including union dummies for low-union (firms with coverage less than .30), middle-union (with coverage from .30 to .60), and high-union (with coverage .60 or greater) companies. Nonunion is the omitted reference group. Year dummies are included in all specifications.

Sample sizes are limited owing to missing data on annual R&D expenditures and the R&D stock, particularly for the earlier years. No distinction can be made in the data set between missing and zero R&D (see Bound et al. (1984) on this issue). For the analysis in this chapter, we have constructed a predicted R&D stock intensity variable, (R&D-STK/S)^{est}, equal to the actual value for those firms with reported values, and equal to the predicted value for companies without such data but with information on its patent stock. The predicted R&D stock intensity variable is calculated based on coefficient estimates from an auxiliary regression of R&D-STK/S on linear, squared, and cubed variables measuring the patent stock divided by deflated sales, plus year and industry dummies. The regression had a sample size of 4,547 and R^2 of 0.42. Regression results are presented both for the larger sample sizes using actual and predicted values of the R&D-STK/S stock intensity variable (columns (3), (4), (3'), and (4')), and for smaller sample sizes wherein R&D-STK/S measures firms' actual stocks (columns (1), (2), (1'), and (2')).[7] The R&D stock is divided by S rather than by the physical capital stock, since the latter is included in q and thus might lead to coefficient bias owing to mismeasured capital on both sides of the equation.

Prior to examining union effects, the relationship of profitability with other variables in table 4.1 is noted. R&D intensity, measured by the estimated real R&D stock divided by (constant dollar) sales, has a positive and significant impact on market value, but is negatively related to the current accounting profit rate. This apparent anomaly may result because current R&D expenditures (which are highly correlated with the R&D stock measured here) lower current earnings, but raise expected future earnings and the market value of the firm. Previous studies have found a negative relationship between accounting profits and R&D divided by sales (Ravenscraft 1983). The R&D-STK/S coefficient is highly sensitive to inclusion of the industry dummies, but relatively insensitive to sample. The log of the capital-labor ratio is included as a control variable in the profitability equations. It is negatively related to q and π_k, indicating decreasing marginal returns to capital or measurement error in the capital stock variable.[8]

. Profitability measure π_k is not found to be significantly related to company size, as measured by $\log(L)$, while Tobin's q is found to increase moderately with respect to size, *ceteris paribus*. Firm-specific two-year growth rates in sales are found to be positively related to current accounting profits, but not to the market valuation of the firm's assets, after accounting for other determinants of q.[9] We also considered the relationship between advertising and profitability. In work not shown, an advertising intensity variable, ADV/S, is positively and significantly related to profitability in regressions excluding industry dummies, but less significant in regressions including industry dummies. To avoid a significant reduction in sample size, advertising is not considered in empirical work presented in the monograph.

Industry-level variables are also found to affect firm profitability. I-GROWTH, the annualized growth rate in real industry sales between years t and $t-4$, is positively and significantly related to all profit rate measures, even after accounting for firm-specific sales growth. The industry concentration ratio (I-CR4), measuring the percentage of sales accounted for by the four largest firms in the assigned industry, is positively and significantly related to both profitability measures. The share of U.S. firms in domestic sales, I-DOMSH, is positively related to profitability measures when industry controls are excluded, but this relationship is not significant in specifications with industry controls (20 dummies to account for 21 industry categories). Industry dummy variables capture any otherwise unmeasured differences in profit determinants that vary systematically across broad industry categories. Their inclusion in the profit equations also can be argued on statistical grounds; the industry dummies are jointly significant by all standard criteria.[10]

We now turn to results on the firm-level union coverage variable, *UN*. By any measure, union firms have significantly lower market valuation and profit rates than similar nonunion firms, although the magnitude of the estimated differentials displays some sensitivity to specification. Comparing nonunion to union firms with 42.3 percent coverage (corresponding to mean coverage among *unionized* companies), coefficient estimates from specifications (4) and (4') indicate that q and π_k are lower by an average 20 and 14 percent, respectively, in union firms than in nonunion firms.[11] The magnitude of the estimated union profit effect is even larger when 2-digit industry dummies are *excluded*, suggesting that union coverage is higher among firms in less profitable *industries*. Note that this evidence need not be inconsistent with the theoretical prediction that unions are most likely to organize *firms* where there exist above-normal monopoly returns or quasi-rents.

In order to check on the robustness of the estimated union effect, specifications also were estimated with 105 industry dummy variables, corresponding to the firms' *Compustat* SIC codes, provided at the 2-, 3-, and 4-digit SIC levels. Following addition of the dummies, the coefficient on UN fell from –0.493 to –0.446 in the log(q) equations, while remaining constant at –0.033 in the π_k equation. Because the union coefficients are not highly sensitive to inclusion of detailed industry dummies, subsequent analysis using industry dummy variables includes only the 20 dummies corresponding to the broader industry categories.

Of particular interest is the fact that the estimated coefficients on firm coverage variable, UN, while sensitive to inclusion of the broad industry dummies, are little affected by inclusion of a measure of industry union coverage, I-UN. This result increases our confidence that we are in fact capturing firm-level union effects on profitability and not unmeasured industry-specific effects correlated with unionization. Industry union density is negatively related to market value, but positively related to current accounting profit rates. Such relationships are consistent with high industry union density decreasing industry output, increasing product price, and improving *current* profitability, while at the same time having a negative effect on the market valuation by investors of firms' assets (due, perhaps, to a greater threat of union organizing). The sensitivity of estimated coefficients on I-UN to sample, specification, and profitability measure, however, makes us reluctant to draw any inferences about the relationship between industry coverage and firm profitability. Moreover, in results not shown, there was extreme specification sensitivity of estimated union coefficients when the CPS-based industry union measure is used as a proxy for firm coverage (i.e., when I-UN but not UN is included). This reinforces our prior conclusion that a firm-level measure of union coverage is strongly preferred to industry measures.

Union Profitability Effects by Industry and Year

In addition to the pooled time-series/cross-sectional analysis presented above, the profitability equations are estimated separately by broad industry category and by year. We first examine union-nonunion differences in profitability within 19 broad 2-digit industry groupings. In order to facilitate presentation, three broad industry groupings—miscellaneous consumer goods, miscellaneous manufacturing not elsewhere classified, and conglomerates—have been combined into a single industry grouping. To the best of our knowledge, industry differences in union profit effects have not been examined prior to this project (for related analysis, see Hirsch 1991).

Table 4.2 provides estimates of the union coverage coefficients from $\log(q)$ and π_k regressions, using as alternative coverage measures the proportion of a company's workforce covered by collective bargaining agreements, UN, and a union coverage dummy variable, UN-DUM, equal to one if $UN \geq .10$ and 0 otherwise. The alternative measures are used because sample sizes of firms and variability in union coverage are limited within some industry groupings. Because estimated union effects proved sensitive to the union measure in some cases, alternative

Table 4.2
Union Profitability Effects by Industry, 1968-1980

Industry	log(q) equations					log(π_k) equations				
	n	UN	|t|	UN-DUM	|t|	n	UN	|t|	UN-DUM	|t|
All manufacturing	6,248	-0.493	(15.87)	-0.226	(12.39)	6236	-0.033	(13.74)	-0.017	(12.26)
Food & kindred products	597	-0.213	(2.78)	-0.197	(3.56)	597	-0.029	(4.56)	-0.027	(5.98)
Textiles & apparel	293	-0.199	(1.90)	-0.049	(0.79)	293	-0.028	(3.87)	-0.008	(1.82)
Chemicals, excluding drugs	423	-1.103	(8.07)	-0.499	(5.99)	423	-0.054	(5.99)	-0.040	(7.59)
Drugs & medical instruments	350	-0.544	(2.45)	-0.262	(3.41)	349	-0.049	(3.01)	-0.017	(2.96)
Petroleum refining	286	0.061	(0.49)	-0.032	(0.55)	286	-0.034	(4.18)	-0.010	(2.50)
Rubber & miscellaneous plastics	225	-1.063	(7.67)	-0.417	(4.32)	225	-0.048	(5.41)	-0.004	(0.71)
Stone, clay & glass	239	-0.059	(0.54)	-0.200	(2.09)	239	-0.031	(4.85)	-0.034	(6.27)
Primary metals	437	-0.713	(6.61)	-0.309	(2.49)	436	-0.036	(4.90)	-0.021	(2.58)
Fabricated metal products	320	0.068	(0.55)	-0.001	(0.01)	320	-0.007	(0.88)	-0.013	(2.49)
Engines, farm & const. equip.	274	0.048	(0.26)	-0.037	(0.36)	273	0.026	(1.96)	-0.007	(1.01)
Office, computers & acct. equip.	177	-3.723	(5.24)	-0.478	(3.48)	177	-0.050	(0.84)	0.005	(0.47)
Other machinery, not electric	412	-0.865	(9.25)	-0.630	(10.78)	409	-0.057	(6.82)	-0.051	(9.91)
Electrical equip. & supplies	414	-0.187	(0.85)	0.085	(1.17)	412	-0.050	(2.50)	-0.007	(1.08)
Communication equipment	276	-0.525	(3.37)	-0.523	(4.94)	276	-0.012	(1.07)	-0.004	(0.46)
Motor vehicle & trans. equip.	403	-0.709	(6.46)	-0.280	(3.68)	401	-0.041	(4.06)	-0.008	(1.16)
Aircraft & aerospace	119	-0.007	(0.07)	0.078	(1.47)	119	-0.006	(0.41)	0.004	(0.50)
Professional & scientific equip.	213	-1.016	(3.51)	-0.382	(2.95)	213	-0.043	(2.63)	-0.018	(2.44)
Lumber, wood & paper	431	-0.778	(7.58)	-0.428	(7.66)	429	-0.056	(5.51)	-0.035	(6.45)
Misc. manufac. & conglomerates	359	-0.335	(3.34)	-0.032	(0.50)	359	0.007	(0.97)	0.013	(2.84)

NOTE: Control variables in industry-specific regressions include R&D-STK/S^{est}, log(L), log(K/L), GROWTH, I-GROWTH, I-CR4, I-DOMSH, and year dummies. The all-manufacturing regression also includes I-UN. The variable UN-DUM=1 if UN $\geq$ .10.

estimates are presented. The top row of table 4.2 presents union coefficient estimates for the entire sample, taken from regressions including both 2-digit industry dummies and industry union density, I-UN. The remainder of the table presents estimated union effects by industry grouping, based on regressions with firm and industry control variables, but not industry dummies or industry union density (the latter varied little across firms within some of the industry categories).

The results reveal substantial variability among industries in the impact of unions on firm profitability. We ignore the results for miscellaneous manufacturing goods and conglomerates (the bottom row), since firms within that category differ so extensively that comparisons have little meaning. No evidence is found for sizable or significant *positive* effects of unionization on profitability in any of the industry categories. There is little evidence, however, of negative union effects on profitability in the fabricated metal products; engines, farm, and construction equipment; electrical equipment; and aircraft and aerospace industry categories. And in the textile and apparel; petroleum refining; office, computer, and accounting equipment; and communication equipment categories, statistically significant negative effects are found for one, but not the other, measure of profitability.[12] Evidence of negative union profit effects is relatively clear-cut in the remaining industries, with particularly sizable impacts found in chemicals; rubber and plastics; primary metals; nonelectric machinery; motor vehicles and transportation equipment; professional and scientific equipment; and lumber, wood, and paper.[13]

Although some of the interindustry variability in estimated union profit effects is due to relatively small sample sizes of companies within broad industry categories, it is implausible that this is the primary explanation for these differences. It is, of course, not surprising that union effects on profitability differ among industries, given that there are substantial differences in bargaining power, labor relations, and union effects on productivity and wages across industries. Unfortunately, it appears difficult to discern a clear-cut pattern in the estimated union effects. Many of those factors that might explain differences in union power—industry concentration, import penetration, firm capital intensity, firm and industry growth, and the like—are already accounted for in the regressions. And in a set of profitability regressions including the union variable and year dummies, but not other control variables, estimated union-nonunion differentials in profitability were not systematically higher or lower than the estimates presented above where detailed control variables are included. Providing an explanation for the sizable inter-industry differences in union profit effects thus poses an important and possibly fruitful avenue for future research.

Union-nonunion profitability differences by year are examined next. The primary advantage of the pooled time-series/cross-section regressions used to this point is the substantial increase in sample size and efficiency associated with pooled analysis. Separate annual regressions, however, also provide significant advantages. First, separate annual regressions avoid the statistical problems of positively correlated error terms (within firms across years) and biased standard errors inherent in the pooled model.[14] Second, annual regressions can help us apprise the degree of measurement error in UN. Union coverage is estimated at a single point in time—thus, measurement error should bias downward its coefficients as one moves away from 1977. Findings to the contrary would suggest that our 1977 union measure provides a reasonable measure of coverage over time. Finally, allowing the union coefficient (as well as others) to vary by year provides evidence as to how union-nonunion differences in profitability have varied over time. Such evidence is of considerable interest and has not been examined previously. For example, a finding that union-nonunion profitability differences were decreasing over time might suggest union bargaining power had weakened and that future contraction in the size of the unionized sector will slow. By contrast, large or increasing profit differences at the end of our period might suggest continued financial pressure on firms' union operations. Alternatively, changes in union profit effects over time can be interpreted in a macroeconomic context, although such an effort would be highly speculative.

Table 4.3 provides a summary of the coefficients on the union variable from the $\log(q)$ and π_k equations, estimated by year. The top line provides estimates from the pooled model, with year dummies (corresponding to estimates presented previously in table 4.1, columns (4) and (4')).

Table 4.3
Union Profitability Effects by Year, 1968-1980

Year	log(q) equations			π_k equations		
	UN coeff.	$|t|$	n	UN coeff.	$|t|$	n
1968-1980	-0.493	(15.87)	6,248	-0.033	(13.74)	6,236
1968	-0.401	(3.46)	359	-0.031	(2.65)	359
1969	-0.525	(3.52)	289	-0.045	(3.42)	289
1970	-0.447	(3.81)	470	-0.035	(3.65)	470
1971	-0.467	(3.94)	499	-0.027	(3.36)	499
1972	-0.610	(4.72)	514	-0.030	(3.85)	514
1973	-0.582	(4.74)	531	-0.038	(4.83)	531
1974	-0.354	(3.55)	552	-0.021	(2.63)	552
1975	-0.528	(4.94)	555	-0.025	(3.69)	555
1976	-0.441	(4.63)	572	-0.031	(4.01)	572
1977	-0.427	(5.15)	553	-0.026	(3.51)	553
1978	-0.385	(4.52)	531	-0.033	(4.13)	531
1979	-0.464	(5.16)	485	-0.028	(3.68)	480
1980	-0.473	(4.06)	338	-0.031	(3.90)	331

NOTES: Annual regressions include R&D-STK/S^{est}, log (L), log (K/L), GROWTH, I-GROWTH, I-CR4, I-DOMSH, I-UN, and IND dummies. The pooled regression includes these controls and year dummies.

The annual estimates are from an identical model, minus the year dummies. The estimates from both sets of equations display reasonable stability across time—there is no clearly evident secular pattern in the union profit effect.[15] The demonstrated intertemporal stability of the estimated union effects provides support for relying on estimates from the pooled models presented in table 4.3.

Interpretation of the annual regression results is not altogether clear. It appears that union coverage significantly reduces companies' earnings and market values, and the magnitude of this detrimental effect has varied little over time. A reasonable interpretation of this evidence is that in response to the large and continuing union tax on profits, there has been a sizable expansion in nonunion operations and a concomitant decrease in the extent of union coverage among U.S. companies. We will return to this theme subsequently. There is the suggestion that union-nonunion differences were particularly large during 1972-1973, years in which stock market values in mean q were also very high. This result is consistent with a hypothesis of union rent-sharing in which unions tax profits at a higher *rate* during good years. Union rent-sharing in profits also is consistent with the hypothesis of risk-shifting from stockholders to labor (Becker and Olson 1989).

An alternative interpretation of the annual results is that the union variable is proxying some other important determinant of profitability, and that this omitted factor has had a stable effect over time. Although this latter possibility cannot be dismissed out of hand, it is difficult to identify what this omitted factor might be. And there is no reason to expect that the effect of this omitted determinant of profitability would have had a constant effect over a 13-year period. We would, of course, have greater confidence in our intertemporal results were union coverage measured throughout the period, and not just in 1977.[16]

Union Rent-Seeking and the Sources of Union Gains

Extant empirical evidence has shown clearly that unionization is associated with significantly lower profitability among U.S. firms and industries. Although there is general agreement that unions reduce profits, there is no consensus as to the *sources* from which unions appropriate gains.[17] On the one hand, some authors (Freeman 1983; Salinger 1984; Karier 1985) have contended that monopoly profits associated with industry concentration provide the principal source of union gains, whereas Clark (1984) has found that unions reduce profits principally among companies with *low* market shares. Hirsch and Connolly (1987) have challenged both sets of results. They soundly reject the notion that industry concentration provides a source for union gains, based both on the absence of such evidence from their firm-level data set and on labor market evidence indicating that union-nonunion premiums are, if anything, somewhat *lower* in more concentrated industries. They provide evidence suggesting that returns associated with R&D capital, market share, and, possibly, limited foreign competition, provide more likely sources for union rents.

The relatively rich data set employed in this study provides a good opportunity to reexamine these unsettled issues. The general specification of the profit model, shown as eq. (4.1), provides for inclusion of variables interacting union coverage with selected explanatory variables. The interpretation of a coefficient on an interaction variable is that it measures union-nonunion differences in that variable's effect on firm profitability. For example, a positive coefficient on concentration and a negative coefficient on a union-concentration interaction term would indicate that industry concentration is associated with higher profitability in companies with low union coverage, but that concentration contributes less to profitability as coverage increases. In general, negative coefficients on union interaction variables would be consistent with a union rent-seeking model in which unions tax some portion of the returns associated with profit-enhancing characteristics.

We estimate two versions of eq. (4.1), the first in which UN enters only as a separate variable, and a second in which UN is interacted with all the right-hand side variables, apart from the 2-digit industry and year dummies. As stated above, the coefficients on the interaction terms provide tests as to how the impact of each of the firm and industry determinants of profitability differs with the extent of firm-level union coverage. Although a simple union tax model would predict that union firms have flatter profiles relating profitability to *all* profit-enhancing firm and industry characteristics, it is likely that unions are more successful at capturing the returns from some profit determinants than from others. Hence, union interaction coefficients are allowed to vary freely across the right-hand side variables.[18]

Table 4.4 presents regression results for the $\log(q)$ and π_k equations. The first column under each profitability measure (columns (1) and (1′)) presents regression results in which a single union variable, UN, but not interaction terms are included (these estimates were presented previously in table 4.1, columns (4) and (4′)). The adjacent columns present regression results from equations with a full set of interaction terms. The *F* statistics presented in these columns test the null hypothesis that the union slope interactions equal zero; in both cases, the null is rejected using standard criteria.

First examined is the extent to which industry monopoly power, proxied crudely by industry concentration, increases firm profitability, and the extent to which these returns are captured by union labor. In a number of past firm-level studies, industry concentration has not been found to be a significant determinant of profitability; indeed, it has often been negatively rather than positively related to profitability (Bothwell, Cooley, and Hall 1984).[19] In this data set, however, industry concentration is positively related to $\log(q)$ and π_k. The hypothesis that monopoly profits associated with concentration provide a significant source of union gains implies that the coefficient on CR should be positive and that on UN•CR negative. That is, CR would significantly increase profitability for nonunion companies, but not for highly unionized companies since unions would capture a share of the above-normal returns associated with monopoly power.

For both the $\log(q)$ and π_k equations there are large *positive* coefficients on UN•CR, implying that concentration, if anything, increases profitability *more* in highly unionized firms than in nonunion firms. These findings are consistent with labor market evidence indicating smaller union-nonunion wage differentials among workers in more concentrated industries. This is strong evidence against the hypothesis that monopoly profits associated with industry concentration provide an

Table 4.4
Profitability Regression Results, With and Without Union Interactions

Variable	Dependent variable – $\log(q)$			Dependent variable – π_k		
	X_i (1)	X_i (2)	UN•X_i	X_i (1')	X_i (2')	UN•X_i
UN	-0.493 (15.87)	0.469 (1.11)	--	-0.033 (13.74)	0.116 (3.57)	--
R&D-STK/S^{est}	0.185 (2.22)	0.685 (6.51)	-2.646 (7.72)	-0.034 (5.34)	-0.032 (3.99)	-0.017 (0.65)
$\log(L)$	0.023 (4.68)	0.029 (3.90)	0.002 (0.13)	-0.00 (1.32)	-0.001 (2.18)	0.002 (1.76)
$\log(K/L)$	-0.058 (3.87)	-0.012 (0.56)	-0.123 (2.71)	-0.008 (7.32)	-0.004 (2.65)	-0.011 (3.12)
GROWTH	0.008 (0.45)	0.034 (1.35)	-0.078 (1.37)	0.006 (4.61)	0.009 (4.90)	-0.010 (2.37)
I-GROWTH	1.301 (8.74)	1.883 (8.99)	-1.837 (4.06)	0.103 (9.08)	0.132 (8.19)	-0.085 (2.46)
I-CR4	0.380 (7.09)	0.163 (1.96)	0.678 (3.91)	0.021 (5.11)	0.011 (1.72)	0.025 (1.87)

I-UN	-0.428 (5.95)	-0.012 (0.11)	-0.497 (9.03)	-0.176 (2.15)	-0.006 (1.22)	0.031 (4.11)	-0.008 (2.02)	0.014 (2.16)
IND	no	yes	no	yes	no	yes	no	yes
YEAR	yes	yes	yes	yes	yes	yes	yes	yes
$\bar{R}^2$	0.332	0.468	0.382	0.480	0.132	0.225	0.149	0.217
n	4,257	4,257	6,248	6,248	4,248	4,248	6,236	6,236

NOTES: $|t|$ in parentheses. Below are coefficients ($|t|$) obtained substituting union dummies for UN in equations (4) and (4′), with nonunion the omitted reference group and where UN-LOW = 1 if ($0 <$ UN $\leq .30$); UN-MED = 1 if ($.30 \leq$ UN $< .60$); and UN-HIGH = 1 if (UN $\geq .60$).

(4): -0.217 UN-LOW - 0.396 UN-MED - 0.371 UN-HIGH.
        (9.68)   (16.92)   (14.85)

(4′): -0.015 UN-LOW - 0.028 UN-MED - 0.026 UN-HIGH.
        (9.01)   (15.52)   (13.65)

important source for union gains. Rather, it suggests that union-nonunion profitability differences are most substantial in highly competitive industries.[20]

Although no evidence is found to support the hypothesis that labor unions capture concentration-related profits, evidence does support the hypothesis that unions capture some share of the improved current earnings associated with limited foreign competition. Evidence from the π_k regressions indicates that limited foreign competition (a high domestic share) is associated with higher earnings in nonunion firms, but not in highly unionized firms. The weakness of the relationship between $\log(q)$ and the extent of foreign competition suggests that gains from limited foreign competition among firms in the manufacturing sector are relatively short-lived; despite higher current earnings, investors do not expect these excess returns to continue indefinitely.

Previous empirical evidence in Connolly, Hirsch, and Hirschey (1986), based on a single 1977 sample of Fortune 500 firms, an industry-level measure of union density, and the use of R&D expenditures as a proxy for the R&D stock, suggests that the returns to R&D investment provide an important source for union gains. This conclusion was based on the finding of a negative coefficient on a union-R&D intensity variable in a market valuation equation; that is, R&D investment added less to the market value of a unionized firm than to an otherwise similar nonunion firm.[21] The results from estimation of the $\log(q)$ equation here provide strong support for this hypothesis. The size of a firm's R&D stock, divided by sales, adds significantly less to the market value of a firm as its union coverage increases (as seen by the negative coefficient on UN•R&D-STK/S). These results provide support to the hypothesis that quasi-rents emanating from a firm's innovative capital stock provide an important source for labor union gains. The implications of these findings for subsequent firm investment behavior are explored in the next chapter. As seen previously, a firm's R&D stock is not positively or significantly related to current earnings. Although the union-R&D interaction term is negative in the π_k equation, no inferences can be made from these results alone. The evidence supports only the proposition that the current R&D stock produces higher *future* earnings, and unions are expected to appropriate some portion of the returns from these investments.

In addition to examining the market valuation of R&D capital in union and nonunion firms, the valuation of a firm's patent stock is considered. Connolly, Hirsch, and Hirschey (1986) suggest that innovative capital that can be patented or licensed is less likely to have its returns appropriated by union labor, since the firm can more easily avoid the union tax. In order to examine this hypothesis, the variable PAT/S, measuring a company's patent stock (Body and Jaffe, no date) divided by constant-dollar sales, is added to the profitability equations shown in table 4.4, separately and in interaction with UN (to conserve space, these results are not shown). The interaction term should not be negative if returns from patented innovative capital can be shielded from union appropriation. Consistent with the finding in Connolly, Hirsch, and Hirschey, however, the interaction term is neither negative nor significant, regardless of profitability measure. The absence of a significant union-patent interaction lends credence to the union rent-seeking model outlined earlier wherein the union tax rate varies across different types of tangible and intangible capital.

Union rent-seeking at the expense of returns from long-lived physical capital leads to the prediction of a negative interaction term between union coverage and capital intensity, $UN \bullet \log(K/L)$. The coefficient on this interaction term is negative and significant in both the $\log(q)$ and π_k equations. Although these results are consistent with the hypothesis of union appropriation of the returns from capital, coefficient bias resulting from measurement error in the net capital stock (which is on both sides of the equation), and simultaneity between profitability, capital investment, and unionization, make us reluctant to attach undue weight to these results. Subsequent evidence in chapter 5, indicating lower annual capital investment by unionized firms, however, provides corroborative evidence and support for the union tax model.

Strong evidence is found for a negative relationship between profitability and interactions between unionization and both firm and industry sales growth. Growth-related profits may represent, in part, quasi-rents and disequilibrium returns associated with variable product demand. Results from the π_k regressions indicate that unions tax a significant proportion of the current earnings emanating from faster firm and industry sales growth. The results from the $\log(q)$ regressions indicate that rapid sales growth adds less to the market valuation of union companies than to otherwise similar nonunion companies, supporting a tax model in which union appropriation of earnings is sustained over time and lowers investors' market valuation of the firm. Such results are consistent with, and may help explain, recent trends indicating simultaneous nonunion employment growth and union membership decline *within* industries (Linneman and Wachter 1986; Linneman, Wachter, and Carter 1990). In addition, the results support the proposition of implicit risk-sharing between the union and shareholders. Union gains increase during good times and fall during bad times. This evidence supports the proposition by Becker and Olson (1989) that there is a shifting of risk from shareholders to labor in unionized companies. They base their conclusion on evidence of lower stock market "betas" (a measure of systematic risk) among highly unionized companies.[22]

The effect of industry union density, I-UN, on firm profitability is not clear-cut. Union bargaining power and the size of the union-nonunion wage premium tend to increase with industry density, placing unionized firms at an increasing disadvantage as density rises. Increased density, coupled with threat effects raising wages for nonunion workers, also permit price increases to be more easily sustained (i.e., unions act like a cartelizing device). Thus we would expect increased industry density to be associated with lower profitability for union firms, but either higher profitability or less detrimental density effects for nonunion firms. The coefficients on I-UN and UN•I-UN presented in table 4.4 provide little evidence in support of this hypothesis, the standard errors on the union density variables being particularly large. In results not shown, however, a union dummy U-DUM (equal to one if $UN \geq .10$) is substituted for UN in specifications (2) and (2'). Using this specification, stronger support is found for the hypothesis. In both the $\log(q)$ and π_k equations, coefficients on I-UN are positive and significant, while coefficients on U-DUM•I-UN are negative and significant.

Econometric Qualifications: Correlated Errors, Union Endogeneity, and Fixed Effects

In this section, three potential shortcomings of the previous analysis are examined—positively correlated firm-specific error terms across time, the possible endogeneity of firm union coverage, and omitted firm-specific effects on profitability. Omitted variables affecting company earnings and market value may have similar effects over time. Hence, firm residuals in one year are likely to be positively correlated with firm residuals in subsequent years, biasing downward coefficient standard errors, and possibly biasing coefficient estimates. Correlation of firm residuals is corrected using a two-step estimation procedure (a related procedure is suggested by Bronars and Deere 1989). In first-step regressions, $\log(q)$ and π_k are regressed on all firm and industry variables that vary from year-to-year, year dummies, and firm dummies for each firm (571 dummies corresponding to 572 firms in the estimating sample). Excluded are variables fixed over time in our data set—UN, I-UN, and industry dummies. The coefficients of the dummies are then used as the independent variables in second-step regressions (the excluded reference firm is assigned a value of zero) in which the fixed variables UN, I-UN, and IND are included. Coefficients on UN provide estimates of the union profit effect with unbiased standard errors.

Results from the second-step regressions ($n = 572$) can be compared to previous estimates presented in table 4.1, columns (4) and (4'). The union coefficient ($|t|$) in the second-step $\log(q)$ equation, which includes UN, I-UN, and industry dummies on the right-hand side, is -0.330 (3.41), as compared to -0.493 (15.87) in the single-stage pooled model. Similarly, the union coefficient in the π_k changes from -0.033 (13.74) in the single-stage model presented previously, to $-.025$ (3.60) in the two-stage model. There is the strong suggestion in these results that pooling across years not only biases downward the standard errors, but may also have resulted in too high an estimate of the union profit effect. But even after accounting for bias resulting from simple pooling, estimated union effects remain large and statistically significant.[23]

A potential shortcoming of virtually all empirical studies of union effects on economic performance has resulted from the fact that union coverage is not randomly distributed across firms or industries. If union coverage is determined simultaneously with firm profitability, or if significant determinants of profitability are not controlled for but are correlated with union coverage, estimated union effects are likely to be biased.

It is likely that union organizing is more extensive and successful among firms with larger monopoly profits and quasi-rents from which unions can appropriate gains. Union coverage, therefore, not only affects firm profitability, but firm profitability also affects the level of coverage. Moreover, the direction of bias resulting from simultaneity appears clear. If higher profits lead to greater union coverage, then the negative effect of unionization on profitability is *understated* using ordinary least squares (OLS) estimation (Voos and Mishel 1986). Past attempts to estimate a simultaneous relationship between unionization and profitability have produced two-stage least squares (2SLS) estimates of union profit effects that are even more negative than are estimates obtained from OLS (Voos and Mishel 1986; Hirsch and Connolly 1987).

The primary difficulty in accounting for union endogeneity is that one must identify and measure factors that influence union coverage, but not profitability. That is, there must exist at least one variable that is included in a reduced-form union equation, but reasonably can be excluded from a structural profitability equation. This task is particularly difficult in this study since unionization is measured at the firm-level, and measurable firm-level variables that influence union coverage and have no impact on profitability are not readily available. Nevertheless, we experimented with various choices of instruments and exclusions from the profit equations in order to obtain 2SLS estimates of union profit effects. In all cases, estimated union profit effects were more negative after accounting for union endogeneity.

Table 4.5 presents OLS, 2SLS, and Hausman specification test results for our preferred set of estimates. The Hausman (1978) specification test provides a formal test of the hypothesis that a variable is exogenous. Both the union coverage variable, UN, *and* an instrumental variable,

Table 4.5
Test for Union Coverage Exogeneity

Variable	Dependent variable – log(q)			Dependent variable – π_k		
	OLS (1)	2SLS (2)	exogeneity test (3)	OLS (1')	2SLS (2')	exogeneity test (3')
UN	-0.493 (15.87)	--	-0.446 (13.06)	-0.033 (13.74)	--	-0.031 (12.04)
UN-HAT	--	-0.709 (9.46)	-0.263 (3.23)	--	-0.038 (6.62)	-0.006 (1.01)
$\bar{R}^2$	0.480	0.466	0.481	0.217	0.198	0.217
n	6,248	6,248	6,248	6,236	6,236	6,236

NOTES: $|t|$ in parentheses. Regression equations include R&D-STK/S^{est}, log(L), log(K/L), GROWTH, I-GROWTH, I-CR4, I-DOMSH, I-UN, and YEAR and IND dummies. UN-HAT is the predicted value of UN from a reduced form equation including 105 industry dummies and the above variables, excepting IND.

UN-HAT, measuring predicted union coverage are included in the profit equations.[24] If the instrumental variable is significantly different from zero, the null hypothesis of union coverage exogeneity can be rejected. For both the 2SLS and exogeneity test estimation, a reduced-form union equation that includes 105 industry dummies is first estimated. The detailed industry dummies are in turn excluded from the subsequent profit equation (20 2-digit dummies are included).

Column (1) provides OLS estimates of the union coefficient, column (2) presents the 2SLS estimates, and column (3) presents OLS results when both UN and UN-HAT are included. Examining first the market value equations, it is seen that the OLS estimate is that a firm with average union coverage (UN = .423) has a q about 20 percent lower than the average nonunion firm. Column (2) provides 2SLS results, with UN-HAT included rather than UN. Consistent with expectations, the estimated union effect on profitability is larger after accounting for simultaneity, the coefficient changing from –0.493 to –0.709. Column (3) provides evidence for a Hausman (1978) specification test where the null is that UN is exogenous. Although the null is rejected in the $\log(q)$ equation (the coefficient on UN-HAT is significant), the relative magnitudes of the coefficients and t-ratios on UN and UN-HAT suggest that exogeneity may not be too inappropriate an assumption.

Although there is some evidence for simultaneity between firm union coverage and market value, no evidence is found for simultaneity between unionization and rates of return on capital. Union coefficient estimates from the 2SLS profitability equations are only slightly larger (in absolute value) than with OLS, and the null hypothesis that UN is exogenous cannot be rejected.[25] The difficulty in identifying appropriate instruments to exclude from a profitability equation, however, makes us reluctant to attach much weight to any specific set of estimates using techniques designed to account for simultaneity bias.

An additional source of concern is that omitted determinants of profitability may be correlated with the union coverage variable, thus leading us to mistakenly attribute to unionism the impact of some omitted factor. The primary means by which such a pitfall is avoided is through the inclusion of detailed control variables in all equations. Estimates of union effects have been based on regressions including numerous firm- and industry-level control variables, including firm-specific sales growth and detailed industry dummies (generally 20 2-digit dummies are included, but as seen earlier, the estimated union effect is relatively insensitive to inclusion of 105 2-, 3-, and 4-digit dummies). Inclusion of such detailed control variables in fact may cause an understatement of the true effect of union coverage since some of unionism's impact is likely to occur through, say, slower growth in sales and lower stocks of R&D, while some of the effects captured by detailed industry dummies may be the result of firm and industry unionization rates.

An alternative way to account for omitted firm-specific effects is the use of a fixed-effects or first-difference model. Rather than estimate the profitability equations in levels form, one can estimate changes in profitability as a function of changes in union coverage and other explanatory variables. Any omitted variables whose effects on company profit levels are fixed over time will thus "fall out" of the difference equation.[26] Unfortunately, data requirements for estimation of fixed-effects models are often prohibitive. Data must be available on the same observations for at least two time periods, degrees of freedom are cut in half if there are only two periods, bias resulting from measurement error in variables is magnified in a change equation (Griliches and Hausman 1986), and the length of time between periods must be sufficiently long for there to be a measurable response of the dependent variable to changes in the independent variables, but not so long a period that the model's parameters change significantly.

Estimation of such a model here is made difficult by the absence of repeated observations on firm-level union coverage at different points in time. Union data for both 1972 and 1977 (along with all other necessary variables) are available for 149 companies, however, therefore allowing a fixed-effects model to be estimated for these firms. Regression equations with the change in profitability between 1972 and 1977 as the dependent variable, and the change in union coverage and in all other explanatory variables during the same period, are estimated.[27] Unfortunately, estimates from these equations provide little information. Estimated coefficients on the change in union coverage variables are close to zero with large standard errors. The models estimated have extremely poor explanatory power and do not allow one to draw inferences about union effects on profitability.

Taken at face value, results from the fixed-effects models suggest that true union effects on profitability are small and that the significant negative effects previously estimated (both here and in all other studies) result from omitted variable(s) positively correlated with unionism and negatively with profitability. Such a conclusion is unfounded, however, in the absence of suspect omitted variables that could possibly account for such large union-nonunion differences in profitability observed in a cross section. No such suspect has been identified. Moreover, the estimated fixed-effects model has a number of deficiencies that are likely to account for the absence of a relationship between changes in union coverage and profitability. First, sample size is relatively small. More fundamentally, the union coverage measures are from different surveys and initially measured different things (the 1972 response measured the proportion of a company's *production* workers covered; this figure was converted to an estimate of companywide coverage). The 1977 measure was collected in 1987-1988 and thus also may contain a fair degree of measurement error. Measurement error in levels is compounded when constructing a difference variable; that is, the ratio of noise to true variation in union coverage is extremely high, biasing the union change coefficient toward zero (Freeman 1984; Griliches and Hausman 1986).

An additional source for concern in the fixed-effects model is that there is likely to be simultaneity between *changes* in profitability and *changes* in company union coverage between 1972 and 1977. Companies with improving profit performance may be more likely to attract union organizing efforts and less likely to attempt cutbacks among their unionized workers. Positive effects of profitability growth on union growth may partially or fully offset negative effects of union growth on profitability growth. On the other hand, firms with improving profit performance may be more likely to expand and build new facilities, many (or most) of which are likely to be nonunion. This bias would work in the opposite direction, leading to an exaggeration of any deleterious union effects. Neither theory nor data is so rich that these relationships can be separated and identified in a reliable fashion. Future research utilizing this study's figures on 1977 *and* 1987 union coverage promises to provide more reliable evidence on the relationship between changes in profitability and changes in union coverage.

Conclusions

The results presented in this chapter provide evidence broadly supportive of the union tax model, whereby unions appropriate a share of the returns from profit-enhancing firm and industry characteristics. Union coverage at the firm level exhibits a strong negative relationship with company earnings and market value, even after controlling in detail for firm and industry characteristics. Average union effects on profitability have been relatively stable over the 1968-1980 period. Differences across 2-digit industries in the union profit effect are substantial, however, and do not lend themselves to simple explanation. The evidence strongly rejects the hypothesis that monopoly profits associated with industry concentration provide a source for union gains. By contrast, evidence is provided suggesting that unions capture current earnings associated with limited foreign competition, both current and future earnings associated with disequilibrium or growing firm and industry demand (sales growth), future earnings emanating from R&D capital, and current and future quasi-rents emanating from long-lived physical capital.

The poor profit performance of unionized companies during the 1970s may provide an important explanation for the marked decline in union membership during the 1980s. As noted by Linneman, Wachter, and Carter (1990) and others, employment declines have been concentrated in the unionized sectors of the economy; nonunion employment has expanded even in highly unionized industries. Although important, shifts in industry demand are an insufficient explanation for the marked decline in private sector unionism. The evidence presented here supports the thesis that declines in union membership and coverage in no small part have been a response to the continuing poor profit performance of unionized companies throughout this period.[28] In subsequent chapters, the implications of union rent-seeking on firm investment behavior, productivity, and productivity growth are explored.

NOTES

1. Lazear (1983) provides a model in which firms that can prevent union organizing at a low cost will be nonunion, and firms that have high prevention costs will be unionized. Although *marginal* union and nonunion firms will have equivalent profit rates in equilibrium, union firms will on *average* have lower profit rates than nonunion firms.

2. Becker and Olson (1987) and Addison and Hirsch (1989) provide surveys and analyses of the profit and market value studies.

3. Several studies examine the effect of strikes on market value. For a review, see Becker and Olson (1987). Interesting as well is the detailed analysis by Abowd (1989b), who finds that unanticipated changes in labor contracts are offset roughly dollar-for-dollar by opposite changes in market value. Abowd interprets these results as supporting the case for ''strongly efficient'' bargaining outcomes, wherein the union and firm maximize the joint value of the enterprise (market value plus worker rents), and bargain over division of the surplus. Note that Abowd's results imply unions are nondistortionary, given the firm's capital stock. His results do not imply that unions have no effect on firms' investment decisions.

4. The ratio of current earnings to equity may differ with respect to union status due to differences in debt financing, risk, or life-cycle earnings among companies with equivalent present values. For example, if union companies shift earnings to the present and rely heavily on debt (Bronars and Deere 1991), they may have a higher earnings-equity ratio than nonunion companies. Or if shareholder risk (beta) is lower in unionized firms (Becker and Olson 1989), earnings-equity ratios and accounting rates of return will be lower (and market valuation of assets higher) than in otherwise similar nonunion firms.

5. The dependent variable $\log(q)$ rather than q is employed as the dependent variable on theoretical and statistical grounds. Based on estimates using the Box-Cox transformation to compare functional forms, and the Jarque-Bera test for normality, the semilog form of the q equation is found to be strongly preferred to the linear (Hirsch and Seaks 1990). Derivation of the multiplicative semilog model is shown in Hirsch and Seaks.

6. Firm-specific labor costs cannot be directly measured for most companies in our sample. It is therefore difficult to estimate how much of the union effect on profitability is due to differences in labor costs.

7. Because R&D-STK/S is bounded below by zero, Tobit model estimation of its predicted value would be preferable to use of ordinary least squares. It is unlikely that estimates of union profit effects are sensitive to the estimation method used for the R&D intensity proxy.

8. Measurement error can lead to a spurious negative correlation since capital is included in the denominator on the left-hand side and in the numerator on the right-hand side. In order to lessen the potential for such bias, the lagged value of the log of the capital-labor ratio was used as an instrument; however, results are highly similar to those presented in table 4.1.

9. The coefficient on GROWTH is significant in $\log(q)$ equations in which firm-year observations with extreme values of GROWTH are omitted from the sample.

10. As discussed below, more detailed industry dummies (105 versus 20 dummies) at the 2-, 3-, and 4-digit levels are also included. Estimated union coefficients are affected little. Subsequent tables in the monograph providing separate estimates by industry category show 19 rather than 21 industry groupings, owing to a merging of the miscellaneous consumer goods, miscellaneous manufacturers not elsewhere classified, and conglomerates categories.

11. In results not shown, the corresponding figure for the rate of return on sales is 12 percent. Mean π_k is .103 for *nonunion* companies. Letting ψ represent the estimated coefficient on union coverage, the average percentage effect of union coverage on profitability is calculated by $(.423\psi/.103)\,100$ for π_k, and by $[\exp(.423\psi)\text{-}1]100$ for q.

12. The evidence suggests that union firms in the relatively high-tech computing and communication equipment industry categories do not have significantly lower current earnings than otherwise similar nonunion firms, but market valuations of the unionized firms' assets, as measured by Tobin's q, are significantly lower. In contrast, union companies in the relatively mature textile and apparel and petroleum industries display significantly lower current earnings, but little difference in market valuation of assets.

13. Interestingly, Clark (1984, p. 912) reports an interindustry pattern of union *productivity* effects not dissimilar from the profitability pattern reported above. Broad industry categories reported here to have weak or uncertain profit effects tended to have positive estimated productivity effects in Clark's analysis, whereas industries found here to have sharply lower profits were reported by Clark to have negative productivity effects. We examine empirically the links between the profitability and productivity evidence more directly in a subsequent chapter.

14. A firm with higher than predicted profitability in one year (i.e., a positive error term) is likely to have higher than predicted profitability the following year. Standard errors in the pooled model, therefore, will be biased downward. A two-step estimation procedure is employed below that utilizes data for all years, but avoids the problem of correlated firm error terms across years.

15. Some variability in estimated coefficients results because the sample of firms changes slightly across years.

16. An omitted variable we can identify is company age, which is positively related to union coverage and negatively related to profitability. Subsequent research incorporating company age into the analysis reveals that it is a significant determinant of profitability, but that its inclusion causes the UN coefficient estimate to decline (in absolute value) by a rather small amount. For an analysis including an age variable, see Hirsch (1991).

17. For an interpretation of this literature, see Addison and Hirsch (1989).

18. Collinearity among the union interaction terms, however, causes some degradation in statistical results and makes precise estimation of the union interaction coefficients difficult. An alternative specification would be to estimate a nonlinear model in which a single union tax parameter is estimated (Salinger 1984; Hirsch and Connolly 1987). Such a model, however, provides little insight as to the sources from which union gains are captured.

19. Ravenscraft (1983) has argued that industry concentration has acted as a proxy for firm market shares, and that it is the latter rather than the former that is positively associated with profitability. In industry-level studies, concentration is almost always positively related to industry price-cost margins.

20. Hirsch (1990b) provides evidence on unions, profitability, and market structure using a smaller sample of companies for which measures on firm market share and industry concentration, weighted to reflect firm sales across industry categories, are available. He finds no evidence to support the proposition that either industry concentration or firm market share provides a source for union rents. Union effects on profitability appear to be most detrimental among companies with low market shares in highly competitive industries.

21. Similar evidence recently has been presented in Bronars, Deere, and Tracy (1989) and Becker and Olson (1990).

22. In work not reported here, we confirm with these data the Becker-Olson result of a negative correlation between beta and union coverage in 1977.

23. Use of weighted least squares (WLS) estimation, where observations are weighted by the inverse of the standard error of the firm dummy coefficients, produces similar results.

24. Because UN is bounded below by zero (and above by one), a Tobit rather than OLS reduced-form estimate would be more appropriate. It is unlikely that this approach would alter our qualitative results.

25. Hirsch and Connolly (1987), using a 1977 firm sample and a union variable measuring the extent of industry coverage, find an identical pattern.

26. Inclusion of a constant in a difference equation accounts for changes in the intercept of the levels equations over the two periods. Note that a difference model is similar to a model in which variables are expressed as deviations from means.

27. Industry dummies fall out since they do not change over the period. They can be included on empirical grounds to account for industry-level difference in profitability change, holding constant changes in other independent variables. The changes in union coverage coefficients are not significant with or without industry dummies.

28. The conclusion here that large union-nonunion *profitability* differences help explain declining unionization is complementary to the conclusion reached by Freeman (1988), Linneman, Wachter, and Carter (1990), and others that high union *wage* premiums have accelerated unionism's decline. It is worth noting that direct evidence linking changes in unionization to changes in profitability has not been provided.

5
Labor Unions
and
Firm Investment Behavior

In the previous chapter, union rent-seeking has been shown to reduce current earnings and the stock market valuation of company assets. In response to the union appropriation of some portion of quasi-rents, unionized companies are expected to reduce investment in tangible and intangible capital relative to their nonunion counterparts. Differences in investment behavior between union and nonunion companies are predicted even where there are strongly efficient contracts maximizing the joint present value of union plus shareholder wealth. As developed in chapter 2, union myopia, owing to the political structure of the union and the nontransferability of union membership, may cause the union to press for current contract gains at the expense of investment and future employment growth. Evidence of differences in investment behavior would indicate that union representation and contract coverage provisions are distortionary, with real effects on resource allocation.

In this chapter, primary attention is focused on estimation of the effects of union coverage on investment in physical capital and in research and development (R&D).[1] In each section, previous literature is reviewed, prior to turning to new estimates drawn from the empirical analysis of the data set assembled for this study. The robustness of the econometric results are probed in some detail. Additional evidence is used to examine the relationship of union coverage with firms' capital-labor ratios, patent propensity, advertising intensity, and debt-equity ratios.

Union Effects on Capital Investment

The union rent-seeking model developed in chapter 2 explains how a union tax on the returns emanating from relation-specific capital stocks can deter company investment in tangible and intangible capital. The union tax effect (plus scale effects associated with higher wage costs) may offset the substitution effect owing to higher relative labor costs. The net effect of union coverage on firm investment behavior is therefore an empirical question. Surprisingly, there is only scant empirical evidence exploring union investment effects. Bronars and Deere (1989) match industry union coverage data to firm observations and find that firms in highly unionized industries have lower capital investment, capital-to-labor ratios, R&D investment, and advertising expenditures. Hirsch (1990a) utilizes 1972 union coverage data for 315 companies and provides evidence showing that union companies have lower physical capital investment than do similar nonunion firms. And Clark's (1984) evidence from lines of business suggests that union coverage has little effect on capital-labor ratios.

Union rent-seeking is likely to affect firm investment behavior both directly and indirectly. The union tax on the returns or quasi-rents to nontransferable capital will *directly* decrease investment as firms decrease investment in order to equate their marginal post-union tax rate of return with their marginal financing cost (see chapter 2). In addition, union rent-seeking will have an *indirect* effect on investment. Lower current earnings due to the union tax will typically produce higher marginal financing costs, thus leading to a further decrease in investment. In this chapter, differences between union and nonunion firms in their investments in physical capital and R&D are examined, with more limited attention given to union effects on other aspects of firm behavior. Because we are interested in how unionism affects current investment, we focus on investment flows or, in other words, additions to the stock of capital and innovative activity (capital *stocks* are controlled for on the right-hand side of the equation).

Profit-maximizing levels of investment are determined by, among other things, firm output and relative factor prices. We estimate double log models in which input variables measuring employment and the capital stock are included on the right-hand side. Output is some linear combination of these included input variables. Alternatively, output (or scale) can be accounted for by estimating investment *intensity* equations in which both sides of the equation are divided by sales (estimates of intensity equations are provided in table 5.5).

We are unable to construct a variable measuring directly capital costs facing the individual firm. Firms within the same industry should face largely similar capital costs. To the extent that capital costs differ among firms with equivalent measured characteristics, we have no reason to expect these differences to be correlated with union coverage. Therefore, an explicit measure of capital costs is not essential, given adequate control for industry and selected firm characteristics. Year dummies will account for economywide cost differences over time. Because retained earnings may provide a lower cost source of funds, we include current firm profitability as a regressor.

A direct measure of labor costs facing the firm is available only for a small number of our firms, but we are able to include a measure of industry labor costs. Although necessitated by data availability, the inclusion of an industry rather than firm wage rate may be appropriate. To the extent that unions affect investment through changes in wage costs, inclusion of a firm-specific wage would be misleading since it would capture much of what is in fact a union effect. Moreover, bargaining models predict that the output and factor mix of union companies is a function of the opportunity cost (industry) wage rather than the "own" wage (chapter 2).

Capital investment equations take the general form:

(5.1) $\log(\text{INV})_{it} = \Sigma \beta_k X_{kit} + \tau \text{UN} + e_{it}$.

INV_{it} represents investment in physical capital by firm i in year t, X_{kit} includes k independent variables (including a constant) affecting investment, and e_{it} is an error term with assumed zero mean and constant variance. Included in X are firm-level variables measuring current earnings, firm size, capital and R&D stocks, and firm sales growth; industry variables measuring concentration, sales growth, import penetration, the wage level, and industry union density; and industry and year dummies.

Regression results for capital investment equations, with the log of annual real investment expenditures, log(INV), as the dependent variable, are presented in table 5.1. Results are presented for specifications with and without industry dummies and the profitability measure, π_k. The direct union effect on investment is measured by τ, the coefficient on UN in eq. (5.1). As shown below, the indirect union effect, operating through a reduced profit rate, is estimated by combining the UN coefficient previously estimated in a profits equation (chapter 4) and the coefficient on the profit measure estimated in eq. (5.1).

The empirical evidence presented in table 5.1 indicates that firm-level union coverage, measured by UN, is negatively and significantly related to capital investment. In addition to the full regression results presented for the three specifications including UN, the note to the table presents the coefficients attaching to categorical union variables in a specification where three dummies are substituted for a continuous coverage variable (UN-LOW=1 if $[0<UN<.30]$, UN-MED=1 if $[.30 \leq UN < .60]$, UN-HIGH=1 if $[UN \geq .60]$, and nonunion is the omitted reference group). Focusing on column (3), the estimated coefficient $(|t|)$ on UN is -0.142 (4.41), implying that an average unionized firm, which in our sample has UN=.423, has annual capital investment about 6 percent lower than a similar nonunion firm.

Coefficients on the categorical variables in the note to table 5.1 suggest a more negative union effect on investment, ranging from 7 to 14 percent. Surprisingly, investment is not found to decrease continuously with respect to union coverage. Rather, deleterious union effects are found to be largest among companies with medium coverage, and somewhat smaller among companies with low and high coverage.

The union coefficients provide estimates of the direct effect of unionization on capital investment, resulting from the union tax on quasi-rents that make up the normal return to investment. In addition, unions have an indirect effect on investment by decreasing the earnings which provide what may be a lower cost source for funding investment than reliance on the capital market.[2] The direct plus indirect effect of unions on annual capital investment can be estimated by:

$$(5.2) \quad d\log INV/dUN = \partial \log INV/\partial UN|_\pi + (\partial \log INV/\partial \pi)_{UN}(\partial \pi/\partial UN)$$
$$= -.142 + (5.212)(-.033) = -.314$$

Table 5.1
Capital Investment Regression Results

Variable	(1)	(2)	(3)
UN	-0.192 (5.91)	-0.299 (8.75)	-0.142 (4.41)
π_k	5.213 (30.25)	--	5.212 (30.40)
log(R&D-STK)^{est}	-0.041 (5.34)	-0.005 (0.54)	-0.012 (1.44)
log(L)	0.068 (4.47)	0.200 (10.84)	0.142 (8.16)
log(K) (-1)	1.023 (82.10)	0.863 (50.50)	0.931 (57.81)
GROWTH	0.045 (4.83)	0.054 (5.69)	0.038 (4.29)
I-GROWTH	0.014 (8.83)	0.014 (8.70)	0.009 (5.79)
I-log(EARN)	0.397 (8.58)	0.351 (4.61)	0.365 (5.13)
I-CR4	-0.002 (3.41)	-0.001 (2.28)	-0.003 (4.60)
I-DOMSH	0.003 (2.80)	0.005 (3.24)	0.005 (3.54)
I-UN	-0.146 (2.49)	0.192 (2.09)	0.110 (1.28)
IND	no	yes	yes
YEAR	yes	yes	yes
$\bar{R}^2$	0.916	0.913	0.924
n	6,232	6,232	6,232

NOTES: Dependent variable is log(INV). $|t|$ in parentheses. Below are coefficients ($|t|$) obtained substituting union dummies for UN in equation (3), with nonunion the omitted reference group and where UN-LOW = 1 if ($0 <$ UN $\leq .30$); UN-MED = 1 if ($.30 \leq$ UN $< .60$); and UN-HIGH = 1 if (UN $\geq .60$).

(3): $-$ 0.073 UN-LOW $-$ 0.145 UN-MED $-$ 0.091 UN-HIGH
     3.15)   (5.92)   (3.49)

where $\partial \log INV/\partial UN|_\pi$ and $\partial \log INV/\partial \pi_{UN}$ are obtained from the coefficients on UN and π_k in table 5.1, column (3), and the estimate of $\partial \pi/\partial UN$ is obtained from the UN coefficient in table 4.1, column (4'). The estimates imply that a typical unionized firm (UN = .423) will have capital investments about 13 percent lower than an otherwise similar nonunion firm. Approximately 45 percent of this total is a direct union effect, while 55 percent is an indirect effect owing to unionism's impact on the firm's current profitability.[3] Note that the total differential of −0.314 corresponds closely to the estimated union coefficient of −0.299 (8.75) in the investment equation specification with π_k excluded (column (2) of table 5.1). Thus, comparison of investment equations estimated with and without π_k included (columns (2) and (3)) provides a relatively simple way to differentiate between unionism's direct and indirect effects.

Results other than those concerning union coverage can be briefly examined. The lagged capital stock variable, $\log(K)(-1)$, acts as a scale variable, with a coefficient close to unity (the log of INV/K could alternatively have been employed as the dependent variable). The positive coefficient on $\log(L)$ indicates that larger companies have higher investment rates, *ceteris paribus*, while no relationship is found between capital investment and the R&D stock. Both firm and industry sales growth, intended to proxy demand shifts, are positively and significantly related to current capital investment. The variable I-log(EARN), measuring average industry labor compensation in a firm's principal 2-, 3-, or 4-digit industry, is a crude proxy for differences in per unit labor opportunity cost facing the firm, independent of company-specific union coverage. As expected, capital investment is positively related to labor costs. Industry concentration is negatively related to firm investment, while limited import penetration (a high I-DOMSH) is associated with greater company investment. Industry union density (I-UN) is positively, but weakly, related to company investment levels in specifications including industry dummies.

The robustness of the union-investment results is probed in several ways. These include the addition of 105 2-, 3-, and 4-digit industry dummy variables to the pooled investment equation, by estimation of investment equations disaggregated by 2-digit industry, and through use of a two-step estimating procedure that purges within-firm serial correlation and its accompanying standard error bias.[4]

Because investment varies significantly across industries, independent of union coverage, highly detailed industry dummies are included to examine the robustness of union coefficient estimates. Inclusion of 105 2-, 3-, and 4-digit industry dummies has little effect, however, changing the coefficient ($|t|$) on UN from –0.142 (4.41) in column (3) of table 5.1, to –0.148 (4.38) (the latter result is not shown in the table). The insensitivity of the union coverage coefficient to the addition of detailed industry increases one's confidence in the robustness of the previously presented results. Because of the relative insensitivity of estimates to inclusion of the detailed dummies, subsequent regressions only include dummies corresponding to the broader 2-digit industry categories.

Table 5.2 presents union effects estimates from investment equations disaggregated for 19 2-digit industry groupings (the category Miscellaneous Manufacturing and Conglomerates combines three categories—miscellaneous consumer goods, miscellaneous manufacturers, and conglomerates—for which separate 2-digit dummies are included in regression estimates). Because industry sample sizes are small and the distribution of union coverage differs enormously across industry categories, estimates are provided with alternative union coverage measures, the continuous coverage variable UN and a union dummy variable, UN-DUM, equal to 1 if UN > .10. Separate coefficient estimates are provided for UN and UN-DUM, and for specifications with and without the inclusion of π_k. Our expectation is that union investment effects vary considerably across industries, just as do union effects on wages, profitability, and productivity. The results in table 5.2 confirm that expectation. Union coverage has negative effects on investment in most industries, but there are substantial differences across industry groupings. Estimates are sensitive to the measure of union coverage (UN versus UN-DUM) and there is variability in the relative importance of direct and indirect union effects. Although some union coefficients are positive and several are close to zero, in no industry

Table 5.2
Union Effects on Investment by Industry, 1968-1980

Industry	n	log(INV) equations w/π_k				log(INV) equations w/o π_k			
		UN	$|t|$	UN-DUM	$|t|$	UN	$|t|$	UN-DUM	$|t|$
All manufacturing	6,248	-0.142	(4.41)	-0.138	(7.38)	-0.299	(8.75)	-0.221	(11.16)
Food & kindred products	597	-0.027	(0.30)	-0.188	(2.75)	-0.176	(1.79)	-0.320	(4.42)
Textiles & apparel	293	-0.026	(0.23)	-0.080	(1.27)	-0.178	(1.51)	-0.113	(1.70)
Chemicals, excluding drugs	422	-0.207	(1.55)	-0.078	(0.95)	-0.489	(3.58)	-0.307	(3.82)
Drugs & medical instruments	349	-0.499	(3.47)	-0.059	(1.20)	-0.668	(4.43)	-0.126	(2.43)
Petroleum refining	286	-0.461	(2.50)	-0.275	(3.31)	-0.542	(3.04)	-0.300	(3.66)
Rubber & miscellaneous plastics	225	-0.507	(3.33)	-0.276	(3.03)	-0.760	(4.91)	-0.269	(2.67)
Stone, clay & glass	239	-0.252	(1.65)	-0.234	(1.73)	-0.657	(3.95)	-0.646	(4.54)
Primary metals	436	0.378	(2.49)	-0.033	(0.18)	0.028	(0.17)	-0.178	(0.89)
Fabricated metal products	320	-0.150	(1.21)	-0.210	(2.81)	-0.213	(1.61)	-0.274	(3.48)
Engines, farm & construction equip.	273	-0.100	(0.52)	0.079	(0.75)	0.035	(0.18)	0.065	(0.59)
Office, computers & acct. equip.	177	-0.020	(0.03)	0.026	(0.19)	-0.358	(0.46)	0.029	(0.20)
Other machinery, not electric	409	-0.072	(0.62)	-0.070	(0.89)	-0.293	(2.49)	-0.269	(3.62)
Electrical equip. & supplies	412	-0.106	(0.41)	0.080	(1.00)	-0.334	(1.25)	0.066	(0.79)
Communication equipment	275	-0.350	(2.87)	-0.309	(3.68)	-0.413	(3.12)	-0.335	(3.65)
Motor vehicle & trans. equip.	401	-0.226	(1.53)	-0.265	(2.40)	-0.437	(2.93)	-0.350	(3.05)
Aircraft & aerospace	119	0.133	(0.46)	-0.229	(1.58)	0.136	(0.47)	-0.232	(1.61)
Professional & scientific equip.	213	-0.295	(1.45)	-0.205	(2.35)	-0.403	(1.82)	-0.252	(2.65)
Lumber, wood & paper	429	0.027	(0.20)	0.061	(0.85)	-0.189	(1.36)	-0.090	(1.25)
Misc. manuf. & conglomerates	357	0.183	(1.52)	-0.058	(0.73)	0.218	(1.72)	0.019	(0.23)

NOTES: Industry regressions include log(R&D-STK)^{est}, log(K)(-1), GROWTH, I-log(EARN), I-Growth, I-CR4, I-DOMSH, and year dummies. Variable π_k included where noted. All manufacturing regressions include these controls, I-UN, and industry dummies. UN-DUM=1 if UN $\geq$ .10.

is evidence found for a positive and significant relationship between union coverage and capital investment.

Among those industries where union effects on capital investment appear particularly detrimental are drugs and medical instruments; petroleum refining; rubber and plastics; stone, clay, and glass; communication equipment; motor vehicle and transportation equipment; and professional and scientific equipment. Those industry groups previously found (chapter 4, table 4.2) to have the largest gap between union and nonunion rates of return on capital are here found most likely to have large negative union coverage coefficients in investment regressions excluding π_k. There is little extant evidence with which these results can be compared.[5] Nor do we possess sufficient industry-specific knowledge that might enable us to identify and interpret patterns in the industry findings. Future research providing additional evidence on differences in within-industry union effects on investment behavior, coupled with a systematic explanation for these differences, is essential.

An attempt is next made to account for positively correlated firm-specific error terms across time through the use of a two-step estimation procedure (see chapter 4 for discussion). In a first-step regression, log(INV) is regressed on all firm and industry variables that vary from year-to-year, year dummies, and dummies for each firm (571 dummies corresponding to 572 firms in the estimating sample). Excluded are variables fixed over time in our data set—UN, I-UN, and industry dummies. The coefficients of the dummies are then used as the independent variables in second-step regressions (the excluded reference firm is assigned a value of zero), in which the fixed variables UN, I-UN, and IND are included ($n = 572$). Second-step regression results provide estimates of the union investment effect with unbiased standard errors.

Results from the second-step regression, as presented below in the text, with the firm coefficients from the first step as the dependent variable, can be compared to previous estimates presented in table 5.1, column (3). The union coefficient ($|t|$) in the second-step equation, which includes UN, I-UN, and IND on the right-hand side, is –0.119 (1.23), as compared to –0.142 (4.41) in the single-step pooled model. The coefficient ($|t|$) on industry density, I-UN, is –0.273 (1.06).

Regressing firm effects on union categorical dummies (with I-UN and IND included) produces the following results:

−0.046 UN-LOW − 0.084 UN-MED − 0.125 UN-HIGH.
(0.68)   (1.18)   (1.64)

These results, suggesting direct negative effects of unions on capital investment in the neighborhood of 4 to 12 percent for companies with various levels of coverage, are similar in magnitude to the single-stage pooled estimates presented previously in table 5.1 (weighted least squares (WLS) estimation, with the inverse of standard errors of the firm coefficients as weights, produced highly similar results). Although the large standard errors associated with the second-step estimates make us cautious in placing too much confidence in the precision with which we are able to estimate such union effects, the results do reinforce the general conclusions reached previously.

Union Effects on Research and Development

The union rent-seeking model predicts that unionized firms should invest less in highly taxed investment paths than do similar nonunion firms. Only recently has there been much attention given to possible effects of unions on investment in forms of intangible capital such as R&D. Connolly, Hirsch, and Hirschey (1986) find lower R&D investment intensities (i.e., R&D/sales) among firms in highly unionized industries. More recently, Hirsch (1990a, forthcoming) has provided evidence showing that union companies have lower R&D investment than do similar nonunion firms, a result confirmed by Bronars, Deere, and Tracy (1989), who also use firm union coverage data. Acs and Audretsch (1988) find fewer innovations in highly unionized industries, while Hirsch and Link (1987) find product innovative activity to be less important among a sample of union businesses than among similar nonunion businesses.

Based on theory and past evidence, union rent-seeking is expected to have significant effects on company investments in R&D and other forms of innovative capital. R&D investment equations here take the general form:

(5.3) $\log(\text{R\&D})_{it} = \Sigma \beta_k X_{kit} + \gamma \text{UN} + e_{it}.$

$\text{R\&D}_{it}$ represents annual investment in R&D by firm i in year t, X_{kit} includes k independent variables (including a constant) affecting R&D, and e_{it} is an error term with assumed zero mean and constant variance. Included in X are firm-level variables measuring current earnings, firm size, capital and R&D stocks, and firm sales growth; industry variables measuring concentration, sales growth, import penetration, wage level, and industry union density; and industry and year dummies.[6] The direct union effect on R&D is measured by γ, the coefficient on UN in eq. (5.3), while the indirect union effect, operating through a reduced profit rate, is estimated by combining the UN coefficient previously estimated in a profits equation (chapter 4) and the coefficient on the profit measure estimated in eq. (5.3).

Table 5.3 presents pooled regression results for R&D investment equations, based on the sample of firms for which R&D expenditure data are reported directly. The dependent variable is the logarithm of real annual expenditures on R&D.[7] Specifications are presented with and without inclusion of industry dummies and π_k.

The coefficients associated with firm union coverage (UN) measure the direct union effect and indicate that unionization significantly decreases R&D investment. The UN coefficient in column (3) implies that a typical unionized company with 42.3 percent union coverage will have R&D investment about 15 percent lower than a similar nonunion company, holding constant π_k and other R&D determinants. There is evidence, however, that the negative union effect on R&D investment varies little with the *extent* of union coverage. Using categorical coverage dummies (seen in the note to table 5.3), even low levels of coverage are associated with significantly lower R&D investment, but the marginal impact of higher levels of coverage is modest. Based on the categorical coverage variable coefficients, unionized companies are found to have R&D investment 23 to 30 percent lower than nonunion companies (calculated by $[\exp(\alpha_i)-1]100$, where α_i are the union dummy coefficients).

Table 5.3
R&D Investment Regression Results

Variable	(1)	(2)	(3)
UN	-0.392	-0.429	-0.378
	(8.69)	(9.45)	(8.36)
π_k	2.534	--	2.031
	(12.08)		(9.81)
log(L)	0.433	0.348	0.334
	(20.51)	(14.08)	(13.64)
log(K)	0.021	0.215	0.228
	(1.19)	(9.01)	(9.64)
log(R&D-STK) (-1)	0.601	0.507	0.508
	(57.24)	(45.18)	(45.75)
GROWTH	-0.019	0.013	-0.007
	(1.18)	(0.81)	(0.48)
I-GROWTH	0.010	0.006	0.005
	(4.92)	(2.80)	(2.17)
I-log(EARN)	1.032	0.734	0.700
	(15.49)	(7.08)	(6.82)
I-CR4	-0.003	-0.005	-0.005
	(5.10)	(5.74)	(5.56)
I-DOMSH	-0.009	-0.005	-0.006
	(5.58)	(2.71)	(3.26)
I-UN	-0.635	-0.303	-0.364
	(7.98)	(2.34)	(2.85)
IND	no	yes	yes
YEAR	yes	yes	yes
$\bar{R}^2$	0.889	0.898	0.900
n	4,327	4,327	4,327

NOTE: Dependent variable is log(R&D). $|t|$ in parentheses. Below are coefficients ($|t|$) obtained substituting union dummies for UN in equation (3), with nonunion the omitted reference group and where UN-LOW=1 if $(0 \leq .30)$; UN-MED=1 if $(.30 \leq UN < .60)$; and UN-HIGH=1 if $(UN \geq .60)$.

(3): - 0.261 UN-LOW - 0.313 UN-MED - 0.351 UN-HIGH.
    (8.60)   (9.66)   (9.82)

The coefficient on UN in column (3) (or on the categorical coverage variables) may understate the true direct effect of unionism, since past unionization has lowered the size of the R&D stock, which in turn lowers current investment. In addition, unions decrease investment indirectly via their effects on the firm profitability, measured here by π_k. The *total* effect of unionism on R&D investment can be measured by:

$$(5.4) \quad d\log R\&D/d UN = \partial\log R\&D/\partial UN_{|\pi} + (\partial\log R\&D/\partial\pi)_{|UN}(\partial\pi/\partial UN)$$
$$= -.378 + 2.031(-.033) = -.445$$

where $\partial\log R\&D/\partial UN_{|\pi}$ and $\partial\log R\&D/\partial\pi_{|UN}$ are obtained from the coefficients on UN and π_k in table 5.3, column (3), and the estimate of $\partial\pi/\partial UN$ is obtained from the UN coefficient in table 4.1, column (4'). These results indicate that most (about 85 percent) of unionism's effect on R&D investment is direct; indirect effects via changes in firms' earnings are relatively small. Note that the union coefficient from a regression without π_k included (column (2) of table 5.4) provides a good approximation of the direct plus indirect union effect.

Coefficient estimates on variables other than union coverage are also of interest. The lagged R&D stock variable, log(R&D-STK)(-1), in conjunction with the capital stock and log of employment variables, acts to control for scale and firm size. All three have positive and significant coefficients, although that on log(R&D-STK)(-1) is well below unity.[8] Industry, but not firm, sales growth is positively related to current R&D investment. As expected, R&D investment is positively related to labor costs, proxied by I-log(EARN). R&D investment appears to be stimulated by competition. R&D investment is negatively related to industry concentration, while vigorous foreign competition (a low I-DOMSH) is associated with larger investments in R&D. Industry union density (I-UN) is negatively related to company R&D investment.

The robustness of the union-R&D results is investigated in a manner analogous to that employed previously for capital investment. Results are examined following the addition of 105 2-, 3-, and 4-digit industry dummy variables to the pooled investment equation, by estimation of R&D investment equations disaggregated by 2-digit industry, and through use of a two-step estimating procedure that purges within-firm serial correlation and standard error bias. As in the case of capital investment, inclusion of detailed industry dummies has little effect on estimated union effects on R&D, changing the coefficient ($|t|$) on UN from –0.378 (8.36) in table 5.3, column (3), to –0.365 (7.90) (not shown in the table). The relative insensitivity of estimated union effects to inclusion of detailed industry dummies is noteworthy, since R&D opportunities and investment intensities vary so significantly across industry.[9]

Table 5.4 presents union coefficient estimates from R&D investment equations disaggregated for 19 2-digit industry groupings. Separate coefficient estimates are provided for UN and UN-DUM, since the range of firm-level union coverage within some of the industry categories is limited (there are no firms in the stone, clay, and glass category with both positive R&D and union coverage less than 10 percent). Union effects on R&D vary considerably across industries, just as do union effects on capital investment (and wages, profitability, and productivity). Although union coverage has negative effects on R&D in most industries, several positive union coefficients are obtained, including significant estimates in the food, petroleum refining, and rubber and miscellaneous plastics industry categories. Large negative (and significant) estimates of union effects on R&D are found in the chemicals, drugs, office and computing equipment, nonelectric machinery, communication equipment, and lumber, wood, and paper industries. Research providing further evidence on, and explanation for, interindustry differences in union effects on R&D investment is needed.

A two-step procedure is used next to estimate the union-R&D relationship after accounting for positively correlated firm-specific error terms across time. A first-step estimating equation regresses log(R&D) on dummies for each firm (451 dummies corresponding to 452 firms in the estimating sample), year dummies, and all firm and industry variables that vary from year-to-year. Variables fixed over time in our data set—UN, I-UN, and industry dummies—are excluded. The coefficients of the dummies are subsequently employed as independent variables in second-step regressions (the excluded reference firm is assigned a value of zero), in which the fixed variables UN, I-UN, and IND are included. Coefficients on UN provide estimates of the union investment effect with unbiased standard errors.

Table 5.4
Union Effects on R&D by Industry, 1968-1980

Industry	n	log(R&D) equations			
		UN	$\|t\|$	UN-DUM	$\|t\|$
All manufacturing	4,327	-0.378	(8.36)	-0.168	(6.60)
Food & kindred products	365	0.282	(2.15)	0.421	(4.03)
Textiles & apparel	131	-0.456	(1.78)	-0.084	(0.61)
Chemicals, excluding drugs	349	-0.692	(4.79)	-0.218	(2.34)
Drugs & medical instruments	338	-1.470	(9.34)	-0.386	(6.92)
Petroleum refining	178	0.846	(3.76)	0.293	(2.63)
Rubber & misc. plastics	192	0.501	(2.97)	0.042	(0.42)
Stone, clay, & glass	163	0.307	(1.78)	a	
Primary metals	158	-0.678	(1.93)	1.494	(4.42)
Fabricated metal products	188	-0.125	(0.52)	0.072	(0.50)
Engines, farm, & const. equip.	219	-0.177	(1.08)	-0.093	(1.00)
Office, computer, & acct. equip.	184	-2.056	(2.78)	-0.344	(2.59)
Other machinery, not electric	328	-0.983	(8.70)	-0.412	(5.31)
Electrical equip. & supplies	340	-0.114	(0.39)	-0.210	(2.30)
Communication equipment	217	-1.031	(6.83)	-0.695	(6.35)
Motor vehicle & trans. equip.	271	0.084	(0.45)	0.251	(1.95)
Aircraft & aerospace	94	-0.727	(1.77)	-0.062	(0.30)
Professional & scientific equip.	225	-0.371	(1.35)	-0.146	(1.18)
Lumber, wood, & paper	183	-1.096	(5.90)	-0.296	(2.05)
Misc. manuf. & conglomerates	204	0.212	(0.78)	-0.015	(0.10)

NOTES: All industry regressions include π_K, log(R&D-STK)(-1), log(L), log(K), GROWTH, I-log(EARN), I-GROWTH, I-CR4, I-DOMSH, and year dummies. Pooled regressions include these controls plus I-UN and industry dummies. UN-DUM=1 if UN≥.10).

a. UN-DUM=1 (UN≥.10) for all firms in stone, clay, & glass sample.

Results from the final or second-step R&D regression, with the firm coefficients from the first step as the dependent variable, indicate a nonlinear relationship between log(R&D) and union coverage (these results are presented below in the text). The union coefficient ($|t|$) in the second-step equation, which includes UN, I-UN, and IND on the right-hand side, is effectively zero, 0.027 (0.11). By contrast, the coefficient on a single union dummy variable UN-DUM (equal to 1 if UN $\geq$ .10) is estimated as –0.168 (1.16). Regressing firm effects on three union categorical dummies (with I-UN and IND included) produces the following results:

–0.160 UN-LOW – 0.192 UN-MED – 0.057 UN-HIGH.
(0.92)   (1.06)   (0.29)

The second-step estimates, suggesting direct negative effects of unions on R&D investment in the neighborhood of 5 to 17 percent for companies with various levels of coverage, are somewhat lower than single-stage pooled estimates presented previously (WLS results are similar to the two-step OLS). Moreover, the large standard errors associated with the second-step estimates produce concern about the precision with which the union-R&D relationship can be measured. The coefficient on industry union density, I-UN, is approximately –1.0 (with $|t|s$ of about 1.3) in all second-step regressions. Although the overall evidence for the hypothesis that union rent-seeking deters investment in innovation capital remains strong, the fragility of the two-step results is troubling.[10]

Further Results: Union Effects on Investment Intensity, Factor Mix, Patent Propensity, Advertising, and Debt

The results presented in this chapter support the proposition that unionized companies invest significantly less in physical capital and R&D than do similar nonunion companies. The union effect appears to result primarily from a union tax on returns from such investments and, to a lesser degree, from lower earnings in unionized firms. In this section, the partial correlations between union coverage and alternative measures of capital investment, R&D, and other behavioral variables are examined briefly. In table 5.5, we present partial regression results providing estimates of union effects on R&D intensity (R&D/S), measured by R&D expenditures divided by sales; capital investment intensity (INV/S), measured by investment divided by sales; capital intensity (K/L), measured by the ratio of the net capital stock to employment; patent propensity (PAT/R&D-STK), measured by the annual number of patents granted per (million) dollar of R&D stock; advertising intensity (ADV/S), measured by the ratio of advertising expenditures to sales; and the debt-equity ratio (DEBT/EQUITY), measured by the ratio of the age-adjusted book value of debt (Cummins et al. 1985) divided by the market value of the firm (for related evidence on several of these relationships, see Bronars and Deere 1989, 1991).

Table 5.5 presents coefficients on firm union coverage variables measured, alternatively, by the single coverage variable, UN, and by the categorical dummy variables UN-LOW, UN-MED, and UN-HIGH. Some of the behavioral variables treated here as dependent variables may be determined simultaneously with right-hand side explanatory variables. We are reluctant, therefore, to interpret the union coefficient as estimates of unionism's causal effects but, rather, interpret these as partial correlations.

Consistent with the R&D and investment level equation results presented above, R&D intensity (R&D/S) and capital investment intensity (INV/S) are found to be significantly lower in union than in nonunion firms. The magnitude of the estimated union-nonunion differential in R&D intensity is particularly large, suggesting union firms have ratios of R&D to sales .015 to .022 lower than nonunion firms, relative to a mean R&D/S of .024 for this sample of R&D-active firms. Point estimates of union-nonunion differences in capital investment intensity, ranging from -.004 to -.009, are relatively small compared to mean INV/S of .062 for this sample of companies. Further examination of the relationship between unionization and physical capital produces interesting results. Although unionized firms invest less in physical capital than do similar nonunion firms, they are more likely than nonunion firms to be capital intensive, as demonstrated by the positive relationship of

Table 5.5
Union Effects on Selected Behavioral Variables: Partial Regression Results

Dependent variable	n	UN	UN-LOW	UN-MED	UN-HIGH
R&D/S	4,327	-0.025 (6.41)	--	--	--
	4,327	--	-0.016 (5.95)	-0.019 (6.55)	-0.022 (6.90)
INV/S	6,596	-0.012 (5.14)	--	--	--
	6,596	--	-0.004 (2.16)	-0.009 (5.38)	-0.007 (3.92)
K/L	6,602	3.524 (2.84)	--	--	--
	6,602	--	-2.941 (3.31)	-0.532 (0.57)	1.465 (1.47)
PAT/R&D-STK	4,121	-0.585 (0.67)	--	--	--
	4,121	--	1.827 (3.15)	0.445 (0.72)	1.315 (1.90)
ADV/S	3,301	-0.006 (2.84)	--	--	--
	3,301	--	-0.004 (2.53)	-0.005 (3.49)	-0.005 (3.27)
DEBT/EQUITY	5,983	-0.001 (0.01)	--	--	--
	5,983	--	0.271 (2.64)	0.234 (2.18)	0.216 (1.85)

NOTES: All regressions include π_k, log(L), GROWTH, I-CR4, I-GROWTH, I-log(EARN), I-DOMSH, year dummies, and industry dummies. Other firm-level variables included differ slightly across equations. Dependent variables are defined as: R&D/S=annual R&D expenditures divided by sales (defined for R&D-active firms only); INV/S=annual investment expenditures divided by sales; K/L=net inflation-adjusted capital stock divided by employees (thousands 1972$); PAT/R&D-STK=patents granted per year, divided by the R&D stock (in millions of 1972$); ADV/S=annual advertising expenditures divided by sales (defined for advertising-active firms only); and DEBT/EQUITY=value of long-term debt adjusted for age structure, divided by equity value.

union coverage with *K/L*. Coefficients on the categorical union dummies indicate this relationship is nonlinear; it is only highly unionized firms that are more capital intensive than nonunion firms.[11]

We find evidence from the categorical union coefficients supporting the proposition that unionized firms have a higher propensity to license or patent than do nonunion firms, given levels of the innovative capital stock (PAT/R&D-STK). This evidence was examined to test the conjecture by Connolly, Hirsch, and Hirschey (1986) that returns from licensable or transferable innovative activities are less vulnerable to the threat of strike and union appropriation. The relationship between patent propensity and union coverage is highly nonlinear, however, making us cautious in reading much into these results.[12]

Evidence of lower advertising intensity (ADV/S) in high union firms is also found, despite the contention by Connolly, Hirsch, and Hirschey that advertising capital is relatively short-lived and not highly vulnerable to union appropriation (ADV/S results display some sensitivity to specification). Point estimates indicate that companies with medium and high union coverage have advertising intensity ratios about .5 percentage points lower than nonunion companies, relative to a mean of 2 percent for the estimation sample. Finally, we find mixed evidence for a significant relationship between DEBT/EQUITY and union coverage (the debt equation is not well specified and has an R^2 of .024). The debt-to- equity ratio does not increase with the *extent* of union coverage, but is significantly larger among union firms than among nonunion firms (as seen by coefficients on the union categorical dummies). The coefficient estimates are also large, relative to the mean DEBT/EQUITY of .43 for this sample of firms. These results provide only limited support for the theoretical and empirical evidence in Bronars and Deere (1991), where it is argued that union firms maximize shareholder wealth by engaging in relatively higher levels of debt financing than do nonunion firms.

Conclusions

Union appropriation of quasi-rents, which include the normal returns to investment in long-lived fixed capital, significantly affects the investment behavior of unionized companies relative to their nonunion counterparts. Although strongly efficient bargaining outcomes may obtain, implying that unions have no real allocative effects *given* existing stocks of tangible and intangible capital (Abowd 1989b), long-run resource allocation is affected. Efficient bargaining outcomes maximizing the sum of union and shareholder wealth imply lower rates of long-lived capital investment among unionized companies, owing to the relatively high discount rate placed on future returns by current union members who cannot recoup the value of future union membership. Moreover, it is unlikely that long-run efficient bargaining outcomes are realized in most industrial settings. To the extent that bargaining parties engage in short-run opportunistic behavior rather than long-run jointly maximizing behavior, current investment in tangible and intangible capital is likely to be further reduced.

The results presented in this chapter provide evidence of union-nonunion differences in physical capital and R&D investment. It appears that union rent-seeking has significant effects on firm investment behavior. Unionized companies invest roughly 20 percent less in physical capital than do similar nonunion companies. Approximately half of this impact appears to be a direct union effect (holding constant current earnings), owing to the union tax on the future earnings stream emanating from the capital stock, while about half is an indirect effect resulting from the significantly lower current earnings among unionized companies. Union investment effects vary considerably, however, across broad industry categories.

Union companies also invest significantly less in R&D than do their nonunion counterparts. Point estimates of the union effect are sensitive to the measurement of union coverage, but the average effect on unionized companies appears to be at least 20 percent. Most of the union effect on R&D investment is a direct effect; indirect effects resulting from lower earnings among union companies are modest. As is the case for physical capital, union effects on R&D investment vary considerably across industry categories. Besides investing less in R&D and physical capital than do nonunion companies, further analysis shows that union companies have a higher propensity to patent given the level of innovation

(R&D) capital, lower advertising intensity, and higher debt-equity ratios. Each of these relationships provides further support for the union rent-seeking model and the implication that unionization has real effects on investment behavior.[13]

NOTES

1. Hirsch (forthcoming) extends parts of the analysis contained in this chapter.

2. A profitability variable can also be included in an investment equation on the grounds that it proxies product demand shifts. Note that the specifications estimated here already include four-year industry sales growth and two-year firm sales growth variables intended to capture demand shifts.

3. The estimate of $\partial \pi / \partial UN$ using a two-step process described in chapter 4 was -0.025, as compared to -0.033 cited above. Using this lower estimate of the union profit effect, the total differential (eq. (5.2)) equals 0.272, with the indirect effect contributing just under half of the total effect.

4. Results from annual regressions for the years 1968-1980 are not presented. They reveal considerable year-to-year variability in point estimates of union effects on capital investment, along with considerable imprecision in estimating these effects. No secular trend is discernible. A fixed-effects model was estimated for 117 firms with union coverage information for 1972 and 1977. No relationship was found between changes in investment and changes in union coverage. For reasons stated in chapter 4, we have little confidence in coefficient estimates from the fixed-effects model.

5. Hirsch (forthcoming) provides closely related evidence using an expanded sample of companies and alternative specifications, and Abowd (1989a) provides industry-specific estimates of union investment effects. Despite large differences in data and methodology, these two papers report broadly similar results.

6. See the discussion above on inclusion of factor prices in an investment equation. The role of union rent-seeking on R&D investment is discussed extensively in chapter 2.

7. Estimates of union effects on R&D based on a larger sample of firms for which a predicted R&D expenditure variable is the dependent variable, are somewhat lower.

8. The sum of the coefficients on the logs of the R&D stock, capital stock, and employment is about one, indicating that, say, a 10-percent increase in labor, the R&D stock, and the physical capital stock, is associated with about a 10-percent increase in current R&D expenditures.

9. In results not shown, separate annual R&D investment equations for the years 1968-1980 are estimated. The coefficients demonstrate a reasonable degree of year-to-year stability, but are somewhat larger (in absolute value) during 1976-1979.

10. Bronars, Deere, and Tracy (1989) examine the union-R&D relationship, and conclude that firm and industry union coverage have negative and significant effects on R&D investment intensity, supporting the previous finding by Connolly, Hirsch, and Hirschey (1986).

11. Causation between capital intensity and unionization may run more from capital intensity to union coverage than the other way around, since unions are more successful at organizing capital-intensive firms (Hirsch and Berger 1984). An analysis of this simultaneous relationship is beyond the scope of this study.

12. The literature on patents and R&D typically treats the patent-to-R&D ratio as a measure of R&D efficiency; that is, innovative output for given levels of R&D input.

13. An important variable omitted from the analysis in this chapter is company age. It is likely that older companies invest less, *ceteris paribus*, and are more likely to be unionized. Hirsch (forthcoming) includes a variable measuring company age (years since incorporation) and finds it to be negatively related to capital and R&D investment. Estimates of union effects on investment, however, are affected relatively little. Preliminary analysis (whose results are not shown) did not provide clear-cut evidence of union effects on employment or the mix between changes in employment and capital investment, although results were sensitive to specification. (Bronars and Deere (1990) have found that firms respond to union representation elections by lowering employment.) Employment is higher in union than in nonunion firms, but then appears to decrease moderately with the extent of coverage. No evidence was found of a significant relationship between union coverage and a dependent variable measuring the four-year change in the log of employment minus the change in the log of the real capital stock. The possible neutrality of changes in the factor mix between capital and labor with respect to union coverage is, of course, consistent with the proposition of strongly efficient bargaining outcomes. But it is also consistent with the union rent-seeking model presented here. High union wages reflect in part the ability to appropriate some portion of the firm's quasi-rents accruing to long-lived capital. Hence, shifts in the factor mix away from labor and toward capital, as suggested by conventional theory, need not be profit-maximizing.

6
Labor Unions, Productivity, and Productivity Growth

Sizable differences exist among U.S. companies in their earnings, market value, and investment behavior. Previous chapters in this monograph have examined the extent to which these differences are accounted for by the variation in union coverage among firms. The results have been interpreted within the context of a union rent-seeking model in which unions appropriate a portion of the returns accruing from market power and long-lived tangible and intangible capital assets.

In this chapter, differences in productivity and productivity growth among U.S. companies are examined. Neither theory nor previous evidence provides unambiguous predictions as to how collective bargaining affects these crucial dimensions of firm performance. Relatively little evidence has been provided, however, on productivity and productivity growth among wide cross-sections of U.S. companies using firm-level measures of union coverage. Below, a brief development of past theory, methodology, and evidence is presented, prior to turning to new evidence on union effects on productivity and productivity growth.

Union Effects on Productivity and Productivity Growth

There exist widely divergent opinions about unionism's effect on productivity. Recent empirical research on productivity and other union effects in the workplace has been inspired in large part by Freeman and Medoff's collective voice/institutional response view of unions (Freeman 1976; Freeman and Medoff 1984) and the seminal article by Brown and Medoff (1978) concluding that union establishments are significantly more productive than nonunion establishments.[1] The voice/response view emphasizes the potential positive role of unions on productivity in environments characterized by internal labor markets with long-run attachment of workers and firms (typically associated with extensive firm-specific training), worker complementarities or team-work in training and production, and workplace "public" goods such as safety, personnel policies, and hours of operation. Unions provide a potential mechanism for correcting the "market failure" deriving from public goods in the workplace. Unionization does this through increased reliance on collective voice, reflecting the preferences of average workers, as opposed to nonunion reliance on individual voice expressed through entry and exit behavior of marginal workers.[2] A union, it is argued, provides a collective voice that more accurately identifies and communicates worker preferences to the firm and establishes grievance procedures and other formalized governance structures that help to reduce exit (quits) and improve employee morale. Cooperative labor-management relations are a necessary but not sufficient condition for positive productivity effects in union establishments.

The voice/response view of unions stands in marked contrast to the traditional view of economists, portraying unions as a labor market monopolist retarding productivity and productivity growth. Negative union effects are believed to result from wage-induced allocative inefficiency, union work rules, limitations on management discretion and flexibility in promotions and job assignments, and decreased worker incentives due to limitations on merit-based wage dispersion. Despite a litany of anecdotal evidence, careful empirical analyses of the effects of work rules are few; and many that exist are industry-specific. Evidence from the construction industry, where much work has been done, suggests that union work rules reduce productivity rather modestly (Allen 1986). In one of the few economywide estimates, Ichniowski (1984) concludes that union work rules, as proxied rather crudely by contract length, are negatively related to productivity. The considerable attention given to work rules by firms and unions during contract negotiations suggests that their effects are not trivial. Yet in the absence of empirical evidence, little can be said about the direct negative effects of union work rules and limitations placed on management.

The empirical debate has centered not on union effects on allocative efficiency but, rather, whether there is a productivity differential between union and nonunion establishments, given equivalent labor and nonlabor inputs (i.e., technical efficiency). Most studies have followed Brown and Medoff (1978) in employing a variant of the Cobb-Douglas production function

(6.1) $Q = AK^{\alpha}(L_n + cL_u)^{1-\alpha}$,

where Q is output, L_u and L_n are union and nonunion labor respectively, K is capital, A is a constant of proportionality, and α and $(1-\alpha)$ are the output elasticities with respect to capital and labor. The parameter c measures productivity differences between union and nonunion labor. A c greater (less) than unity implies union labor is more (less) productive than nonunion labor. Letting P equal union density (L_u/L), Brown and Medoff approximate eq. (6.1) by:

(6.2) $\log(Q/L) = \log A + \alpha \log(K/L) + (1-\alpha)(c-1)P$.

Eq. (6.2) assumes constant returns to scale, an assumption relaxed by including a $\log L$ variable as a measure of establishment size. The productivity differential of unionized establishments is estimated by the coefficient on P (the coefficient on P divided by $1-\alpha$ provides an estimate of c if the union productivity effect solely reflects the differential efficiency of labor inputs).

Using state-by-industry data for 1972, Brown and Medoff (1978) conclude that union establishments are significantly more productive than nonunion establishments. And subsequent industry-specific studies have provided some additional evidence of positive union productivity effects (see Freeman and Medoff 1984). Addison and Hirsch (1989), however, evaluate extant evidence and conclude that no compelling case exists for a statistically or quantitatively significant positive *or* negative union productivity effect. Previous estimates, they point out, vary considerably across firms and industries and positive productivity effects appear to be in response to decreased profit expectations. This is broadly consistent with a "shock effect" and selectivity interpretation (Addison and Hirsch 1989). Productivity gains are largest where unions acquire sizable wage gains and where there are significant competitive pressures, thus shocking management into increasing productivity. Little evidence is found for positive union productivity effects in the public and not-for-profit sectors. Moreover, union firms whose productivity and profits decrease are most likely to contract in size or go out of business and, therefore, are underrepresented in available data samples. Finally, large positive productivity effects are inconsistent with the evidence on profitability and employment (see Addison and Hirsch 1989, and Wessels 1985, respectively).

There have been few productivity studies using both firm (or line of business) observations from multiple industries and firm (or business-level) measures of unionization. Clark (1984) finds little difference between productivity (sales per unit of labor input) in union and nonunion lines of business. Hirsch (1990a) uses a sample of *Compustat* companies and a 1972 measure of collective bargaining coverage. He finds productivity to be lower among union companies, but estimates are highly sensitive to the inclusion of industry control variables. Recently, Kruse (1988, chap. 3) has estimated production functions for a sample of *Compustat* companies, employing a firm-level union status dummy equal to one if the Bureau of Labor Statistics (BLS) has reported any collective bargaining contract settlements involving the company. He reports moderately higher productivity among manufacturing companies with some union coverage (and substantially higher productivity among unionized nonmanufacturing companies).[3]

There are a number of limitations to the production function test (Brown and Medoff 1978; Addison and Hirsch 1989). The use of value added as an output measure may confound price and quantity effects, since part of the measured union productivity differential can result from higher prices in unionized sectors. In this case, the union coefficient in the production function may crudely track the union-nonunion wage differential.[4] Data limitations may also necessitate the assumption of identical production function parameters in the union and nonunion sectors. And the reliability of the production function test also may depend on the ability to control for all important inputs in the production process, since unmeasured "firm effects" may not be independent of union status.

A serious concern surrounding the union productivity test is that of selectivity. Since union firms (or units of firms) facing higher wage rates must be more productive to survive in the very long run, the productivity effect is not being measured across a representative sample of firms. Rather, only surviving union firms with sufficient productivity increases are likely to be observed, thus causing the union productivity effect on a representative firm to be overstated. Additional concerns are the overly restrictive assumption of Cobb-Douglas technology, and the simultaneity problem between inputs and outputs in OLS estimation of any production function. While these limitations are not addressed here, one response to these latter concerns has been to directly estimate (translog) cost and profit functions (e.g., Allen 1987).

The limitations discussed above will make it necessary to qualify carefully the conclusions based on subsequent productivity evidence. Because several of our reservations apply to omitted or unmeasured determinants of productivity levels, analysis of productivity changes (growth) may purge empirical analyses of fixed effects. Hirsch and Link (1984) show that changes in total factor productivity, ϱ, derived by subtracting $\alpha\log(K/L)$ from both sides of eq. (6.2) and differencing, is a function of changes in union density, dUN. Following the productivity growth literature emphasizing the role of R&D on growth, Hirsch and Link employ a three-factor Cobb-Douglas function that includes technical capital, T. Their total factor productivity growth equation (ignoring control variables) is

(6.3) $\varrho = \gamma + \phi(dT/dt)/Q + (1-\alpha)(c-1)d\text{UN},$

where ϱ is total factor productivity growth, γ is the rate of disembodied growth (the time derivative of $[\log Q - \alpha\log K - (1-\alpha)\log L]$), ϕ is $\partial Q/\partial T$ (the marginal product of technical capital), dT/dt approximates net investments into stock T, and $(dT/dt)/Q$ is proxied by R&D intensity. A positive coefficient on the change in union density, dUN, implies $c > 1$ and supports the voice/response view. Estimating the production function in difference form has the advantage of netting out unmeasured fixed effects, but in this context requires a measure of changes in unionization over a suitably long time period.[5] As seen below, we estimate productivity growth equations, including a union-level variable but not a change variable.

Union Effects on Productivity: Empirical Evidence

In order to examine union effects on productivity, a variant of the Brown-Medoff model is estimated, with labor productivity a function of capital intensity and unionization. We estimate:

$$(6.4) \quad \log(VA/L)_{it} = \Sigma\beta_k X_{kit} + \alpha\log(K/L)_{it} + (1-\alpha)(c-1)UN_i + e_{it},$$

where $\log(VA/L)$ is the log of value added per employee in firm i and year t, $\log(K/L)$ is the log of the capital-to-labor ratio, UN is firm-level union coverage, and X includes k firm and industry determinants of productivity (including an intercept). A positive (negative) coefficient on UN implies that union firms have $c > 1$ $(c < 1)$ and have higher (lower) technical efficiency. Among the variables in X will be the log of labor, $\log(L)$; the log of the R&D stock per employee, $\log(\text{R\&D-STK}^{est}/L)$; the two-year firm-specific growth rate in real sales, GROWTH; the four-year industry growth rate of real sales, I-GROWTH; industry concentration, I-CR; industry share of sales by domestic firms, I-DOMSH; industry union coverage, I-UN; and year and industry dummies. The industry variables and dummies are potentially important since labor productivity varies considerably across industries and time, and unionization is not randomly distributed across industries.

Variables measuring firm and industry growth, industry concentration, import competition, and industry union density are not variables normally included in production function equations. Variables affecting demand growth, product market competition, and union density are likely to affect product price, however, so their inclusion is important in studies using a value added rather than physical output measure of productivity. If these control variables were absent, it is likely that some of the measured differences in value added would result from price rather than output differences. This is particularly critical for measurement of union-nonunion differences in productivity, since union coverage is correlated with growth and product market structure variables.

All variables used in regressions in this chapter are defined in Data Appendix 2. Productivity is measured by value added per worker, where value added represents the approximate difference between company sales and the costs of materials (inventory changes are ignored). Value added is measured with error, however, owing primarily to the absence of data in *Compustat* on the cost of materials. The *Compustat* item "cost of goods" measures materials and production costs, including all labor costs. In order to approximate value added, firm labor costs must be added back in. Approximately a quarter of the firms in our sample had direct measures of labor compensation and pension costs available in *Compustat*, thus allowing a relatively accurate approximation of value added. For the remaining firms, labor costs were estimated by multiplying firm employment times average industry compensation, the latter being inflated by 1.25 times UN in order to reflect the higher labor costs in union firms (were this adjustment not made, there would have been spurious negative correlation between unionism and value added). The 1.25•UN adjustment factor is consistent with a 25-percent labor cost differential and was arrived at through experimentation on the sample of firm-years with actual labor and pension costs. For these firms, mean measurement error (defined as the difference between "actual" value added and "estimated" value added) was less than 1 percent and uncorrelated with union coverage (the simple correlation coefficient is .001). Thus, measurement error in value added should not result in coefficient bias in the productivity level or productivity growth equations.

Production function estimates are presented in table 6.1 for specifications with and without inclusion of industry variables and dummies.[6] The coefficient on UN is found to be negative and significant in all specifications. The magnitude of the union coefficient, however, is sensitive to the inclusion of industry-level variables and dummies. In column (1), the coefficient ($|t|$) is –0.186 (13.76), but falls in absolute value to –0.131 (9.07) when industry variables are included (column (2)). The further addition of 2-digit industry dummies changes the union coefficient to –0.082 (6.10). For a typical unionized company with UN = .423, the point estimate in (3) indicates that factor productivity is about 3.5 percent lower than in a nonunion company. Use of separate union coverage dummies (see the note to table 6.1) indicates a nonlinear union effect, with the most negative effect on productivity being for firms with medium coverage (.30 ≤ UN < .60). These results indicate that

Table 6.1
Productivity Regression Results

Variable	(1)	(2)	(3)
UN	-0.186	-0.131	-0.082
	(13.76)	(9.07)	(6.10)
log(K/L)	0.274	0.266	0.285
	(51.47)	(51.49)	(43.64)
log(R&D-STK^{est}/L)	0.080	0.073	0.038
	(24.30)	(22.80)	(11.20)
log(L)	-0.001	-0.011	-0.013
	(0.41)	(4.55)	(6.07)
GROWTH	0.025	0.020	0.018
	(5.80)	(4.86)	(4.81)
I-GROWTH	--	0.009	0.006
		(13.17)	(9.33)
I-CR4	--	0.004	0.003
		(18.52)	(14.44)
I-DOMSH	--	0.001	0.001
		(2.61)	(2.38)
I-UN	--	-0.051	0.283
		(2.09)	(7.95)
IND	no	no	yes
YEAR	yes	yes	yes
$\bar{R}^2$	0.400	0.450	0.567
n	6,248	6,248	6,248

NOTES: Dependent variable is log(VA/L). $|t|$ in parentheses. Below are coefficients ($|t|$) obtained substituting union dummies for UN in equation (3), with nonunion the omitted reference group and where UN-LOW=1 if $(0 < UN \leq .30)$; UN-MED=1 if $(.30 \leq UN < .60)$; and UN-HIGH=1 if $(UN \geq .60)$.

(3): - 0.020 UN-LOW - 0.065 UN-MED - 0.49 UN-HIGH.
    2.04)   (6.49)   (4.50)

low-, medium-, and high-union coverage firms have factor productivities 2.0, 6.5, and 4.9 percent lower, respectively, than their nonunion counterparts.

As further evidence of the sensitivity of union coefficient estimates to the addition of industry controls, 105 2-, 3-, and 4-digit industry dummies are added to the labor productivity equation, in lieu of the 2-digit dummies and I-UN, which is measured at the 3-digit level (these results are not shown in the tables). Inclusion of these dummies causes the union coefficient ($|t|$) to fall in absolute value from –0.082 (6.10) to –0.030 (2.38). Coefficients ($|t|$) on the coverage dummies become –0.026 (2.90), –0.054 (5.78), and –0.026 (2.58) for the low-, medium-, and high-union dummies, respectively. These estimates, indicating that unionized companies have factor productivities roughly 2.5 to 5 percent lower than nonunion companies, are consistent with Clark's (1984) finding of negative but small (2 to 3 percent) union productivity effects among U.S. lines of businesses during the 1970-1980 period. Our results, in conjunction with the finding that profitability is significantly lower among union companies, provides strong evidence that the frequently cited finding by Brown and Medoff (1978) of large positive union productivity estimates is unique to their data set and should not be generalized. Nor can a compelling case be made from the data assembled here that there exists a large and statistically robust negative effect of unions on productivity.

Coefficients on other variables in the productivity equations are largely as predicted. The coefficient α, on log(K/L), which provides a crude proxy for capital's share in value added, is 0.29. The coefficient on the R&D stock per employee is about 0.04, in line with (or a little lower than) estimates from previous studies (Griliches 1986). There exists weak evidence of diseconomies of scale, based on the negative coefficient on log(L), although measurement error in *Compustat*'s variable measuring number of employees may produce a spurious negative correlation between log(VA/L) and log(L). Firm- and industry-specific growth rates in sales, intended to proxy demand shifts, are positively associated with factor productivity. This relationship may result either from high capacity utilization rates among firms facing strong sales growth (and labor hoarding during downturns), or the presence among growing firms of newer and more productive capital which is not fully reflected in our measures of the capital stock. The variables I-CR and I-DOMSH appear to capture industry effects (e.g., product price effects on value added); the coefficient on each changes from a positive to negative value when 3-digit industry dummies are included (results not shown).

Finally, the positive coefficient on industry union density, I-UN, is consistent with the hypothesis of a positive price effect in industries with high union density. That is, to the extent that a high level of industry union coverage increases product price, measured productivity or value added is higher for both union and nonunion companies. The magnitude of the coefficient is surprising, however, suggesting that I-UN is correlated with (i.e., capturing) omitted determinants of productivity. This increases further our caution in attaching much weight to coefficient estimates on the firm-level union measures.

In addition to examining economywide union-nonunion productivity differences, we also disaggregate results by industry. Although the overall union productivity effect appears to be small, union effects across industries should vary considerably. This expectation is based in part on the considerable interindustry variation observed for union-nonunion differences in wages, profitability, and investment. Union wage and profit effects, for example, should provide a major impetus to management to reduce X-inefficiency and increase measured productivity (Addison and Hirsch 1989). The expectation of highly variable union productivity effects is based as well on the belief that union-nonunion productivity differences result from differences across firms in labor relations and the "institutional response" by management to union representation (Freeman and Medoff 1984).

Table 6.2 provides estimates of union productivity effects by industry category, based on specifications including a single union coverage variable, UN, and the three categorical coverage variables. A considerable degree of variation in union productivity effects across industry categories is found. Note that some of the variation results from the very small number of companies within each industry-by-union category cell. In cases where there are less than two companies in a nonunion or high-union cell (each company is of course observed for multiple years), the dummy variable is collapsed into the next union category variable.

Table 6.2
Union Productivity Effects by Industry, 1968-1980

Industry	n	(1) UN	|t|	(2) UN-LOW	|t|	UN-MED	|t|	UN-HIGH	|t|
All manufacturing	6,248	-0.082	(6.10)	-0.020	(2.04)	-0.065	(6.49)	-0.049	(4.50)
Food & kindred products	597	-0.019	(0.47)	-0.047	(1.15)	-0.101	(2.58)	-0.039	(1.00)
Textiles & apparel	293	0.100	(2.70)	0.074	(2.68)	0.105	(3.53)	0.080	(2.91)
Chemicals, excluding drugs	423	-0.358	(6.71)	-0.037	(0.70)	-0.103	(1.94)	-0.179	(2.66)
Drugs & medical instruments	350	-0.275	(3.91)	-0.044	(1.66)	-0.151	(4.48)	[b]	
Petroleum refining	286	-0.317	(3.16)	[a]		-0.123	(4.21)	[b]	
Rubber & miscellaneous plastics	225	-0.128	(2.60)	0.065	(2.00)	0.033	(0.78)	-0.078	(2.34)
Stone, clay & glass	239	0.112	(2.99)	[a]		0.053	(2.68)	0.049	(2.10)
Primary metals	437	-0.169	(4.20)	[a]		-0.117	(3.72)	-0.105	(3.97)
Fabricated metal products	320	0.233	(6.42)	0.028	(0.73)	0.112	(3.51)	0.165	(5.44)
Engines, farm & construction equip.	274	0.244	(4.16)	-0.013	(0.31)	0.051	(1.33)	0.188	(3.58)
Office, computers & acct. equip.	177	-0.584	(2.45)	-0.195	(6.43)	[c]		[c]	
Other machinery, not electric	412	-0.050	(1.51)	-0.091	(1.51)	-0.081	(3.50)	-0.078	(2.82)
Electrical equip. & supplies	414	-0.386	(4.86)	0.041	(1.54)	-0.173	(4.62)	0.056	(1.45)
Communication equipment	276	0.031	(0.56)	[a]		-0.085	(2.31)	0.183	(5.82)
Motor vehicle & trans. equip.	403	0.055	(1.26)	0.397	(9.77)	0.242	(8.26)	[b]	
Aircraft & aerospace	119	0.044	(0.60)	[a]		0.149	(4.47)	[b]	
Professional & scientific equip.	213	-0.298	(3.94)	-0.206	(6.97)	-0.436	(8.44)	-0.106	(1.99)
Lumber, wood & paper	431	-0.303	(6.52)	0.008	(0.26)	-0.191	(5.20)	-0.171	(4.94)
Misc. manuf. & conglomerates	359	0.221	(5.34)	0.317	(7.30)	0.362	(7.72)	0.406	(8.93)

NOTES: All industry regressions include $\log(K/L)$, $\log(\text{R\&D-STK}^{est}/L)$, $\log(L)$, GROWTH, I-GROWTH, I-CR4, I-DOMSH, and year dummies. Pooled regressions include these controls, I-UN, and industry dummies. UN-LOW=1 if $(0<\text{UN}\leq.30)$, UN-MED $=.30<\text{UN}\leq.60$, and UN-HIGH=1 if $(0<\text{UN}\leq.30)$.

a. UN-LOW combined with nonunion.
b. UN-HIGH combined with UN-MED.
c. UN-HIGH and UN-MED combined with UN-LOW.

Positive union productivity effects are observed for several industries (we ignore the miscellaneous manufacturing and conglomerate category). As previously found by Clark (1984), union companies in the textile and apparel industry have higher productivity than do nonunion companies. Productivity effects are not large enough, however, to prevent somewhat lower profitability among these companies (chapter 4, table 4.3).[7] Positive union productivity effects are found as well among companies in the following industries: fabricated metal products; engines, farm and construction equipment; and motor vehicle and transportation equipment. The latter results must be discounted somewhat since there are a small number of firms in both the nonunion and low-union categories. The other two industries, however, were previously found to have similar earnings and market valuation of union and nonunion firms, indicating that positive productivity effects are sufficient to offset union wage premiums. There is also weak evidence of higher union productivity among companies in the stone, clay, and glass, communication, and aircraft and aerospace industries. The small number of nonunion firms in these industries, however, makes such comparisons difficult.

More widespread evidence is found for negative union productivity effects, although the magnitude and statistical significance of these estimates are small in many of the industry categories. A relatively clear-cut union disadvantage in productivity is found in the following industries: chemicals; drugs; petroleum refining; primary metals; nonelectric machinery; electrical equipment; professional and scientific equipment; and lumber, wood, and paper. This list of industries corresponds closely to the industry categories for which companies are found to have lower profitability and market value (chapter 4, table 4.3). In short, union effects on company profits are most severe in those industries where negative union productivity effects reinforce (or do not offset) union effects on labor compensation.

The productivity equations estimated above assume common slope parameters or output elasticities with respect to capital, R&D, and labor among union and nonunion firms. But as shown by Brown and Medoff (1978), union productivity estimates may be highly sensitive to violations of this assumption. In order to examine the possibility of varying slope parameters, the right-hand variables $\log(K/L)$, $\log(\text{R\&D-STK}^{est}/L)$, $\log(L)$, and I-UN are interacted with UN. The interaction variables permit the effects of these inputs and industry union density to vary systematically with the extent of firm-level union coverage, and allow us to identify the routes through which union-nonunion productivity differences take place. In results not shown, significant negative coefficients are found on the interaction terms of UN with $\log(K/L)$, $\log(\text{R\&D-STK}^{est}/L)$, and $\log(L)$. A positive coefficient is found on the interaction of UN with I-UN.

The lower output elasticities with respect to physical capital and R&D found for highly unionized companies are consistent with Baldwin's (1983) union expropriation model in which union companies rationally invest in "second-best" capital as a means of mitigating union wage demands. The reasoning here is that unions will tend to have a standard rate across establishments within the same company. By maintaining inefficient capital or plants, union demands for wages above the marginal revenue product at the inefficient plants will result in employment losses for the union. What appears clear is that union companies are more likely to be in mature industries and establishments, with older and less productive capital stocks. Although the R&D and physical capital variables are age-adjusted measures, they may not reflect fully quality differences in the capital stocks between union and nonunion companies. The positive coefficient on the interaction of UN with I-UN suggests that productivity or price increases are more likely among union than among nonunion companies in highly unionized industries.

The robustness of the union productivity results are examined further by using a two-step estimation process intended to account for positively correlated firm-specific error terms across time. In a first-step regression, $\log(VA/L)$ is regressed on all firm and industry variables that vary from year-to-year, year dummies, and dummies for each firm (571 dummies corresponding to 572 firms in the estimating sample). Excluded are variables fixed over time—UN, I-UN, and industry dummies. The coefficients of the dummies are then used as the dependent variables in second-step regressions (the excluded reference firm is assigned a value of zero), in which the fixed variables UN (or, alternatively, union category dummies), I-UN, and IND are included (n=572). Second-step regression results provide estimates of the union productivity effect with unbiased standard errors.

Results from the second-step regression (shown in text below), with the firm coefficients from the first step as the dependent variable, cast further doubt on the robustness of the results presented previously. The union coefficient ($|t|$) in the second-step equation, which includes UN, I-UN, and IND on the right-hand side, is –0.014 (0.23), as compared to –0.082 (6.10) in the single-stage pooled model. The coefficient ($|t|$) on industry density, I-UN, is 0.537 (3.30). Regressing firm effects on union categorical dummies (with I-UN and IND included) produces the following results:

0.082 UN-LOW + 0.041 UN-MED + 0.030 UN-HIGH.
(1.90)   (0.92)   (0.63)

These results suggest that productivity is somewhat *higher* among companies with relatively low levels of union coverage than among nonunion and highly organized companies (results using weighted GLS regressions are similar). This pattern is exactly the opposite of that previously found. The positive and significant coefficient on industry union density, I-UN, is relatively insensitive to the measurement of firm union coverage.

The large standard errors associated with the second-step estimates prevents us from placing weight on these specific results. But, likewise, our earlier results must also be discounted owing to the sensitivity of the union coefficient estimates to the addition of detailed industry dummies, the considerable diversity of productivity estimates across industries, the different pattern of union effects found using the two-step estimation procedure, and the known biases and difficulties inherent in the production function methodology (Addison and Hirsch 1989).

In short, the econometric evidence on productivity is simply too fragile to draw strong inferences about union effects in the workplace. That being said, there is no evidence to support the contention of large and statistically significant positive union productivity effects. Based on the relatively clear-cut evidence of lower profits and market values in union companies, we also know that positive union productivity effects are not sufficiently large in general to offset cost increases owing to union wage premiums. Based on the evidence from this study, it can be concluded that union productivity effects are small on average, vary considerably in sign and magnitude across industries and individual workplaces, and cannot be estimated precisely with existing techniques and data bases.

Union Effects on Productivity Growth: Empirical Evidence

The effects of unionization on productivity growth are examined using a variant of eq. (6.3). Rather than compute changes in total factor productivity, "partial" productivity growth rates (Griliches 1986) are calculated. The variable $\varrho_{it, t-4}$ is defined as the annualized logarithmic growth between years t and $t-4$ in deflated value added, minus the growth of employment times labor's share of total cost. The growth rate of capital is included on the right-hand side of the equation. Such a specification is appealing in data sets where capital's share is difficult to estimate accurately. The productivity growth equation takes the following general form:

$$(6.5) \quad \varrho_{it, t-4} = \Sigma\beta_{\varrho k}X_{kit,t-4} + \delta UN_i + e_{t,t-4},$$

where $\varrho_{it,t-4}$ is the growth rate in productivity (as defined above) by firm i between years t and $t-4$, and UN is firm-level union coverage in 1977 with coefficient δ. The vector X includes a constant and firm-level measures of the growth rate of physical capital ($d\log(K)$), the growth rate of the R&D stock or estimated R&D stock ($d\log(\text{R\&D-STK}^{est})$), the average level of the R&D stock in years t and $t-4$ ($\log(\text{R\&D-STK}^{est})$), the growth rate and average level of employment ($d\log(L)$ and $\overline{\log(L)}$), and 2-digit industry dummies. Industry-level variables include union density in 1977 (I-UN), average annual sales growth over the four-year period (I-GROWTH), the average share of sales by domestic firms in an industry during years t and $t-4$ (I-DOMSH), and the average share of energy in total cost during years t and $t-4$ (I-ENERGY/VA). Because we measure firm unionization only at a single point in time, we are unable to estimate the relationship between changes in productivity and changes in unionism.

Table 6.3 presents regression results for the productivity growth equations, with and without inclusion of industry level variables and dummies. In regression models without industry variables, we find that productivity growth is positively and significantly related to the growth rate of physical capital and the level of (but not change in) R&D stocks, but significantly lower among union firms.[8] The UN coefficient in column (1) suggests that unionized firms realize productivity growth substantially lower than do nonunion firms (mean ϱ is .023 for this sample of firms and four-year periods). Once industry-level variables and 2-digit dummies are included, however, the estimated direct union effect on productivity growth falls, from a point estimate of –0.027 in column (1), to –0.011 when industry-level variables (but not industry dummies) are added in (2), and to –0.007 with the further addition of industry dummies in (3). Replacing the continuous union coverage variable, UN, with three categorical variables corresponding to low, medium, and high levels of coverage (see the note to table 6.4), coefficient ($|t|$) estimates of –0.004 (1.96), –0.006 (2.86), and –0.005 (2.30) are obtained for low-, medium-, and high-union coverage firms, respectively. These results indicate that even small levels of coverage are associated with slower productivity growth, but that growth varies little with the *extent* of coverage among unionized companies.

The results strongly suggest that much of the slower productivity growth of union firms during the 1970s was due to industry-level effects independent of unionization. This conclusion is based on the fact that estimated union coefficients become closer and closer to zero as industry control variables are added to the regressions. Yet even in a regression with detailed controls, we find that unionized companies had productivity growth about a half of a percentage point lower than nonunion firms, not a trivial amount relative to a sample average ϱ of 2.3 percent. To check the sensitivity of the estimates to a more detailed control for industry, the productivity growth model is estimated with the inclusion of 105 industry dummies measured at the 2-, 3-, and 4-digit level (these results not shown in tables). It is interesting that the union coefficients do not further decrease (in absolute value) following the addition of detailed dummies, the coefficient ($|t|$) on UN changes

Table 6.3
Productivity Growth Regression Results

Variable	(1)	(2)	(3)
UN	-0.027	-0.011	-0.007
	(9.95)	(3.89)	(2.32)
$d$log(K)	0.107	0.136	0.151
	(8.57)	(11.28)	(13.06)
$d$log(L)	0.270	0.231	0.221
	(20.30)	(17.96)	(18.15)
$d$log(R&D-STK^{est})	0.002	0.001	-0.003
	(0.32)	(0.15)	(0.58)
log(R&D-STK^{est})	0.004	0.002	0.002
	(6.01)	(3.28)	(2.38)
$\overline{log(L)}$	-0.003	-0.001	-0.001
	(352)	(153)	(0.70)
$\overline{\text{I-GROWTH}}$/100	--	0.154	0.130
		(11.78)	(9.90)
$\overline{\text{I-DOMSH}}$/100	--	-0.050	-0.010
		(4.46)	(0.83)
$\overline{(\text{I-ENERGY/VA})}$/100	--	-0.143	-0.030
		(12.69)	(1.79)
I-UN	--	-0.011	0.013
		(2.22)	(1.80)
IND	no	no	yes
YEAR	yes	yes	yes
$\bar{R}^2$	0.335	0.390	0.463
n	4,258	4,258	4,258

NOTES: Dependent variable is $\varrho_{t,t-4}$. $|t|$ in parentheses. Below are coefficients ($|t|$) obtained substituting union dummies for UN in equation (3), with nonunion the omitted reference group and where UN-LOW=1 if (0 < UN ≤ .30); UN-MED=1 if (.30 ≤ UN < .60); and UN-HIGH=1 if (UN ≥ .60).

(3): − 0.004 UN-LOW − 0.006 UN-MED − 0.005 UN-HIGH.
     (1.96)   (2.86)   (2.30)

to –0.008 (2.97), and those on UN-LOW, UN-MED, and UN-HIGH change to –0.005 (2.57), –0.007 (3.53), and –0.006 (2.95), respectively. Thus, the results appearing in table 6.3 appear to provide sufficient controls for industry-specific effects on productivity growth.

Estimates of union effects on productivity growth by industry category are provided in table 6.4. As expected, considerable variability exists and standard errors are relatively large in most cases. In no industry is evidence found for a significant positive relationship between union coverage status and productivity growth. There is at least moderately strong evidence of a negative union effect on growth in the chemicals, drugs and medical instruments, communication equipment, motor vehicle and transportation equipment, and professional and scientific equipment industries. Interestingly, these industries tend to be technologically advanced and have higher than average productivity growth rates and investments in R&D. And although the correlation is not perfect, these industries also tend to be ones where union coverage was previously found to impact negatively on profitability, investment in capital and R&D, and productivity.

Finally, robustness of the productivity growth results is examined by using the two-step estimation process designed to account for positively correlated firm-specific error terms across time. In the first step, ϱ is regressed on firm and industry variables that vary from year-to-year, year dummies, and dummies for each firm (530 dummies corresponding to 531 firms in the estimating sample). The coefficients on the firm dummies then form the dependent variable in second-step regressions in which the fixed variables UN (or, alternatively, union category dummies), I-UN, and IND are included. These second-step regression results (n=531) provide estimates of the union growth effect with unbiased standard errors.

Results from the second-step regression (not shown in tables) indicate a sizable negative relationship between productivity growth and union coverage when industry dummies are excluded. When industry dummies are included, however, the negative relationship between firm productivity growth and union coverage vanishes (weighted GLS regression results are similar). For example, the coefficient ($|t|$) on UN in

Table 6.4
Union Effects on Productivity Growth by Industry, 1968-1980

Industry	n	(1) UN	|t|	(2) UN-DUM	|t|
All manufacturing	4,327	-0.0066	(2.32)	-0.0055	(3.33)
Food & kindred products	407	-0.0046	(0.61)	-0.0064	(1.13)
Textiles & apparel	196	0.0040	(0.43)	0.0017	(0.31)
Chemicals, excluding drugs	287	-0.0193	(1.69)	-0.0213	(3.17)
Drugs & medical instruments	241	-0.0251	(1.91)	-0.0148	(3.53)
Petroleum refining	198	-0.0149	(0.52)	-0.0148	(1.10)
Rubber & misc. plastics	156	-0.0063	(0.55)	0.0036	(0.55)
Stone, clay, & glass	165	-0.0046	(0.46)	a	
Primary metals	305	0.0067	(0.55)	0.0142	(0.98)
Fabricated metal products	219	-0.0109	(1.03)	-0.0080	(1.24)
Engines, farm, & const. equip.	184	-0.0100	(0.80)	-0.0010	(0.15)
Office, computer, & acct. equip.	118	-0.0028	(0.07)	0.0052	(0.73)
Other machinery, not electric	279	-0.0062	(0.70)	-0.0051	(0.88)
Electrical equip. & supplies	275	-0.0293	(1.61)	-0.0029	(0.46)
Communication equipment	188	-0.0193	(1.71)	-0.0186	(2.34)
Motor vehicle & trans. equip.	271	-0.0035	(0.31)	-0.0144	(1.77)
Aircraft & aerospace	83	0.0104	(0.45)	0.0005	(0.05)
Professional & scientific equip.	147	-0.0466	(2.62)	-0.0145	(1.89)
Lumber, wood, & paper	295	0.0032	(0.31)	0.0008	(0.16)
Misc. manuf. & conglomerates	244	0.0168	(1.97)	0.0003	(0.06)

NOTES: All annual regressions include π_k, R&D-STK (−1), log(L), log(K), GROWTH, I-log(EARN), I-GROWTH, I-CR4, I-DOMSH, and year dummies. Pooled regressions include these controls, I-UN, and industry dummies. UN-DUM=1 if UN ≥.10).

a. UN-DUM=0 for only one firm in stone, clay, & glass sample.

a second-step equation with I-UN and industry dummies *excluded* is –0.009 (1.60), but changes to 0.003 (0.51) in the second-step model that includes I-UN and IND on the right-hand side. The evidence presented in this chapter supports the proposition that most of the slower productivity growth associated with union coverage is accounted for by the disproportionate presence of unionization in industries with slower growth. And given the relative fragility of the productivity growth evidence following econometric probing, we are unwilling to reject the proposition that union effects on productivity growth are, on average, close to zero.

Conclusions

Results presented previously in this monograph have shown rather clearly that union coverage in the workplace has significant negative effects on firm profitability and investment behavior. These relationships are interpreted within the context of a rent-seeking model in which unions appropriate some share of the quasi-rents that make up both normal and supra-competitive returns to fixed, long-lived, tangible and intangible capital. In this chapter, we explore differences in productivity levels and productivity growth between union and nonunion companies, *given* their stocks and investments in capital, R&D, and labor.

Neither theory nor previous evidence provides unambiguous predictions as to union effects on productivity levels and growth. Although the initial evidence in this chapter indicates that union coverage is associated with lower productivity levels and slower productivity growth, further probing indicates that these relationships are anything but clear-cut. Much of the union-nonunion difference in performance results from the fact that unions are organized disproportionately in companies and industries with characteristics leading to lower productivity and slower growth, independent of any direct union effects.

Moreover, estimated union effects exhibit tremendous variability across and within industries, not only in magnitude and statistical significance, but also in sign. Admittedly, sample sizes of companies within industry categories are small, but much of the interindustry variability appears to result from real differences in unionism's impact across sectors. While explanation for these differences lies beyond the scope of this research, differences in competitiveness, management and labor relations, financial conditions, and technological opportunities are likely to be important. A final caveat emerges from the fragility of the estimates found when using a two-step estimation process designed to purge firm-specific correlation of error terms across years. Negative relationships of union coverage with productivity and productivity growth are no longer found using this two-step process.

Based on the evidence presented here, we cannot reject the hypothesis that unions, on average, have little direct effect on productivity and productivity growth. Note that this conclusion does not imply that unions do not matter in the workplace. Rather, it implies that unionism's *net* impact, comprised of both positive and negative effects on performance, is generally small. Moreover, attention in this chapter has focused exclusively on unionism's direct impact on economic performance or, more explicitly, on union-nonunion differences in productivity levels and growth for *given* inputs and characteristics. Indirect effects resulting from the union impact on profits, market value, and investments in capital and R&D may be of consequence. That is, even though the union impact on technical efficiency (i.e., output obtained from given inputs) is apparently small, the financial and investment impact of unionism leads to lower levels and slower growth in productivity-related inputs. As discussed previously, absent positive productivity effects that offset union wage increases, decreased profitability leads predictably to lower investment and retrenchment in the unionized sectors of the economy.

NOTES

1. Surveys and interpretations of the unions and productivity literature are available in Freeman and Medoff (1984), Hirsch and Addison (1986, chap. 7), and Addison and Hirsch (1989).

2. While they do not explicitly discuss unions, Williamson, Wachter, and Harris (1975) analyze a similar workplace environment, which they characterize as one of "idiosyncratic exchange." Foulkes (1980) examines personnel policies in large nonunion companies. Freeman and Medoff are skeptical, however, about the possibility of a nonunion solution to the public goods problem.

3. Recent firm- and industry-level studies from the U.K. suggest that British unions (and, in particular, the closed shop) have even more negative productivity effects (for a survey, see Metcalf 1988).

4. Evidence of lower profitability by union firms, however, indicates that firms are limited in their ability to pass price increases forward to consumers.

5. Hirsch and Link find both union level and change variables to be negatively related to productivity growth among 2-digit manufacturing industries. Besides having an extremely small sample size, industry-level analyses do not allow disentangling of union and industry effects on growth.

6. These specifications also were estimated for two smaller samples—those companies with directly measured (i.e., not estimated) R&D stocks, and the sample of companies for which labor compensation, used in the calculation of value added, is reported directly. In the first case, results from the alternative samples were highly similar. In the latter case, estimated union effects on productivity were somewhat larger (more negative) than those reported in this chapter.

7. Addison and Hirsch (1989) conclude that a competitive environment (as in textiles and apparel) is a necessary condition for positive productivity effects to result in response to union wage and profit effects. Kazis (1989) documents how unions and large manufacturers have worked together to modernize and improve productivity in the textile and apparel industries.

8. Results with respect to union coverage are not affected when the equation is estimated for the smaller sample with complete R&D stock information. The coefficients on the R&D variables, however, are larger and more significant than those presented in table 6.4.

7
Summary and Evaluation

This monograph examines the impact of collective bargaining coverage on the economic performance of publicly traded U.S. manufacturing companies during the 1970s. It develops a union rent-seeking model which posits that unions appropriate a share of the returns from market power and from quasi-rents accruing to long-lived capital. Among the performance measures examined are company profitability, market value, investment behavior, productivity, and productivity growth.

As part of this study, a survey of companies was conducted to collect firm-level information on the extent of collective bargaining coverage during 1977 and 1987. Coverage data from this survey are combined with more limited information obtained from a 1972 Conference Board study to create a single firm-level union variable approximating collective bargaining coverage in 1977. Firm union coverage information is then combined with detailed company data for the 1968-1980 period on market value, earnings, sales, capital investment flows and capital stocks, R&D expenditure flows and R&D stocks, patents, employment, advertising, and debt, as well as industry data on concentration, import competition, sales growth, payroll, and union density.

Data collected from the survey indicate substantial interindustry and intraindustry variability in the proportion of workers covered by collective bargaining agreements. Among the 452 companies reporting figures for both 1977 and 1987, collective bargaining coverage averages 30.5 percent in 1977, but declines to 25.0 percent by 1987 (table 3.2). The decline in unionization is widespread, coverage decreasing in all but one of 19 broad industry categories (there is virtually no change in average coverage among companies in the electrical equipment and supplies group). Substantial intraindustry variation in collective bargaining coverage indicates a potentially large benefit from measuring unionization at the firm- as well as industry-level in empirical studies of economic performance.

Examination of variable means, cross-classified with union coverage status, reveals large differences in economic performance between non-union and highly unionized companies (Data Appendix 1). The market valuation of company assets, measured by Tobin's q, and company profitability, measured by the rate of return on capital, decline sharply with respect to union coverage. Investment intensity in innovation capital, measured by the ratio of R&D expenditures to sales and the ratio of patents to sales, shows particularly steep decreases with respect to union coverage. Capital investment intensities, measured by the ratio of annual investment to sales, and advertising intensity, measured by the ratio of advertising expenditures to sales, are similar among nonunion companies and companies with low levels of coverage, but decline among companies with medium and high levels of coverage. Capital intensity, on the other hand, measured by the capital stock per employee, is substantially lower among nonunion than union companies, but varies little with the extent of coverage among union companies. Value added per worker is similar among nonunion and low-union companies, but lower among companies with medium and high coverage levels. Productivity growth, by contrast, declines sharply as one moves from the nonunion to low-union category, and continues to decline as union coverage increases.

In short, descriptive data on variable means for the 1968-1980 period show that the economic performance of unionized companies has been poor relative to the performance of nonunion companies. But simple means cross-tabulated by union coverage category need not match closely the partial correlations of union coverage with performance measures, controlling for other determinants of performance. Differences in means most definitely do not provide evidence as to the causal impact of unionization on the economic performance of firms. That is, unions may be more highly organized in sectors where economic performance is expected to be poorer, independent of any direct role played by collective bargaining coverage. For example, average four-year industry sales growth in firms' principal industry is significantly higher for nonunion than for union firms, leading to greater profitability and market value, investment, and productivity. The primary purpose of the empirical analysis contained in chapters 4-6 is to isolate and measure more precisely the impact union coverage has on firm economic performance.

Estimated Union Effects on Profitability, Investment, and Productivity

Chapter 4 probes in some detail the impact of union coverage on company profitability and market value. By any measure, the negative union impact on each is large. Holding constant detailed firm characteristics, industry characteristics, and industry dummies, Tobin's q is estimated to be about 20 percent lower in an average unionized company than in a similar nonunion company. The corresponding union-nonunion differential for the rate of return on capital is about 15 percent. Estimates of the union profit effect are smaller using a two-step estimation process that corrects for within-firm correlation of error terms across time; estimates are larger using instrumental variable estimation attempting to account for the possible endogeneity of union coverage. Union profit effects are found to be relatively stable over time, but to vary considerably across industries. The data do not allow us to measure directly the exact sources from which unions acquire compensation gains, but estimation of models with union interaction terms suggests that quasirents accruing to capital and R&D, profits associated with changes in firm and industry demand (disequilibrium returns), and returns from limited foreign competition provide the primary sources for union gains. No evidence is found for the proposition that monopoly returns associated with industry concentration provide a source for union gains.

The impact of labor unions on firm investment behavior is the subject of chapter 5, with particular attention to investments in physical capital and R&D. Unions are found to have both direct and indirect effects on investment. The union ''tax'' on the returns to long-lived fixed investment causes a *direct* decrease in the profit-maximizing investment level. The lower profitability resulting from union coverage reduces investment *indirectly* by lowering the internal pool of funds that provides a preferred source for the financing of investments. Regression estimates indicate that the average union firm has annual capital investment that is about 13 percent lower than a similar nonunion firm. Approximately half of this effect is a direct union effect and half an indirect effect working through the union impact on profitability. Estimates of the union investment effect are insensitive to the addition of highly detailed industry dummies to the equation, and relatively insensitive to estimation correcting for serial correlation of within-firm error terms. As expected, the union effect on investment varies considerably across industries, although in no industry do we find a positive and significant relationship between union coverage and capital investment.

Estimates of the union impact on R&D indicate a large negative effect on R&D expenditures, although the estimated magnitude of the union effect displays sensitivity to the estimation method and measurement of union coverage. Even low levels of union coverage are associated with lower R&D expenditures, while extent of coverage among unionized companies has little if any effect. Unionized companies invest about 15-20 percent less than similar nonunion companies, most of this difference being a direct rather than an indirect (profitability) effect. Estimated union-nonunion differences are not affected by the inclusion of detailed industry dummies, but are moderately lower using the two-step estimation procedure that corrects for serially correlated within-firm errors. Substantial differences across industries are found, including positive estimated union effects in two industry categories.

Less detailed analysis is provided for union effects on other behavioral variables (table 5.5). In addition to lowering investment intensities in physical capital and R&D, union coverage is negatively associated with the ratio of advertising expenditures to sales. The propensity to patent (the ratio of patents filed to the R&D stock) is larger among union than nonunion companies, suggesting that union firms are more likely to license innovative capital as a means of protecting quasi-rents from union appropriation (but this relationship is not estimated precisely). And the use of debt relative to equity is higher among union than nonunion companies, consistent with the hypothesis of Bronars and Deere (1991) that efficient contracting between a firm and union leads to a shift toward debt financing. The union impact on the capital-labor mix could not be estimated precisely. This may result from the fact that unions may have a relatively neutral impact on factor mix, reducing both capital investment and employment in roughly equal proportions. Alternatively, it may reflect the fact that capital intensity and union coverage are simultaneously determined, making estimation of the relationship difficult.

In chapter 6, the effects of labor unions on productivity levels and growth are examined. Neither theory nor previous evidence provides unambiguous predictions as to union effects on productivity and productivity growth. Much of the poorer performance by union companies results from the fact that unions are more likely to be organized in firms and industries with lower productivity levels and growth, independent of any direct impact of unionization. Thus, estimates of union productivity effects are relatively sensitive to the inclusion of detailed industry dummies and control variables. In a pooled equation with detailed industry controls and dummies, value added per worker is estimated to be 2 to 5 percent lower in union than in nonunion companies. Evidence also is found to support the proposition that capital and R&D, and to a lesser extent labor, inputs have lower output elasticities (i.e., are less productive) in union than in nonunion companies. But use of a two-step estimation process, intended to purge standard error bias, results in an estimated *positive* but insignificant union-productivity relationship. Based on the varied evidence from chapter 6, it is concluded that union effects on productivity are, on average, rather small.

As expected, there is large interindustry variability in estimated union productivity effects, and large standard errors attach to almost all of the estimates. Roughly, union-nonunion productivity differences are estimated to be positive in those same industries where negative union profit effects are found to be small. Any negative productivity effects appear to be more than offset by the positive effects resulting from collective voice aspects of unions and management response to collective bargaining and union rent-seeking. In contrast, those industries where union firms realize substantially lower earnings and market value exhibit union productivity effects that are negative or close to zero.

The evidence on productivity growth is likewise mixed. Unionized companies exhibit substantially slower four-year productivity growth rates than nonunion companies, but most of this slower growth is the result of unionized companies having firm and industry characteristics that lead to slower growth for union and nonunion firms alike. As was the case for productivity level estimates, a negative union effect is no longer found when using the two-step estimation process. Within-industry differences in productivity growth cannot be estimated with precision. Union effects on productivity growth appear most deleterious, however, among union companies in relatively high-growth, technologically advanced industries.

Interpretation and Qualifications

The evidence presented in this monograph provides broad support for the union rent-seeking model presented in chapter 2. It is argued there that unions appropriate some portion of the returns from market power and from the quasi-rents that make up the normal returns to long-lived capital. Because the time horizon for a union (or its rank-and-file with median preferences) is shorter than the planning horizon over which investors evaluate long-lived capital, "efficient" labor contracts that maximize joint (union plus shareholder) wealth imply lower investment in fixed tangible and intangible capital than would exist in a nonunion company. And if jointly maximizing contractual agreements do not obtain, as is likely, the union tax on quasi-rents and the retardation of investment spending are expected to be even larger.

Unionized companies will reduce investment in vulnerable forms of capital, due not only to the union "tax" that places a wedge between gross and net rates of return, but also because company profits, which provide a pool from which investments are frequently financed, are lower. Union companies, therefore, are expected to exhibit lower current and future profitability, and lower investments in long-lived capital, than their nonunion counterparts. Union rent-seeking need not have any direct effects in the workplace on productivity (i.e., technical efficiency) or productivity growth. But union rent-seeking will reduce output levels and sales growth indirectly through its effect on investment behavior and the use of productive inputs.

Evidence presented here shows clearly that unions have distortionary effects on firm investment behavior that lead to lower input usage and output in unionized sectors of the economy. It is more difficult, however, to draw inferences about union effects on economywide efficiency based on union-nonunion behavioral differences. Lower capital investment among unionized firms can be offset by higher capital investment elsewhere in the economy. If resources could costlessly flow to alternative uses, and social rates of return were equivalent in nonunion sectors, there would be little effect of unions on economywide efficiency. Increases in union power and rent-seeking would simply cause the relative size of the union sector to shrink. But unions could not then have the significant long-run effects on firm profitability that are so clearly observed. Because unions have some degree of monopoly bargaining power, because the shifting of resources from union to nonunion environments occurs slowly, and because social rates of return differ across investment paths, union distortions at the firm level necessarily translate into some degree of inefficiency economywide.

Private-sector unionism has declined sharply in recent years, and nonunion work environments have increasingly become the norm for most of the workforce and in most sectors of the economy (Kochan, Katz, and McKersie 1986; Freeman 1988). It is essential that we better understand the relationship between this transformation in U.S. industrial relations and past union effects on firm performance. The results presented in this monograph strongly suggest that union decline and increased management hostility have been in no small part the direct result of the significantly worse economic performance of union companies than of nonunion companies during the 1970s.[1]

An evaluation of this study must consider several important qualifications about the empirical analyses and results, and it should outline areas of future study that may prove fruitful. Evidence presented here and elsewhere has established that there are significant differences in economic behavior and performance between union and nonunion companies. What is less clear, however, is the extent to which unionization is a causal force, and the exact routes through which union organizing and bargaining power affect firm performance. We have provided a rent-seeking framework in which union effects on profitability, investment behavior, and productivity growth can be analyzed jointly. Yet reservations about this study's findings remain. The most serious statistical and methodological concerns are the possible endogeneity of firm-level union coverage (and other variables as well), selectivity bias engendered by an inability to observe nonsurviving firms, and the difficulty in measuring the dynamic effects of union coverage.

In most of the foregoing analysis, firm-level union coverage generally is treated as an exogenous variable, even though unionization is not randomly distributed across firms and industries, and coverage is affected by profitability and capital intensity (leading to potential simultaneity bias). As seen in chapter 4, it is technically feasible to test for exogeneity using Hausman-type specification tests to account for the endogeneity of key variables, or to estimate a full system of simultaneous equations. Given the limitations of available data and theory, however, we have little confidence in such results. Firm-level information that would help us estimate a reduced-form union equation is not readily available, although industry-level variables on workforce characteristics could be employed. And while all equations could be overidentified by excluding selected variables or through the estimation of nonlinear relationships (or, for example, through the use of stocks in one equation and flows in another), selection of instruments would be largely arbitrary since reasonable arguments can be made that almost any variable affecting, say, R&D, would also affect profitability.

In short, superficial treatment of union endogeneity is unlikely to be helpful, while more detailed treatment is beyond the scope of this study. We are confident, however, that the qualitative relationships found are correct. Many of the biases that can be identified suggest that union effects on economic performance are underestimated. Unions are more likely to be successful in organizing firms with the largest potential profits or quasi-rents; hence the negative union coefficient in the profit equations may *understate* the true negative impact of unions on profits

(Voos and Mishel 1986). Likewise, simultaneity bias between capital and unionization (i.e., unions are more likely to organize in capital intensive industries), may result in an underestimate of the negative effect of unions on capital investment.[2] Working in the opposite direction may be a negative relation between opportunities for R&D investment and union organizing costs. Rapidly growing firms with technological opportunities and large white-collar workforces may be particularly difficult to organize. Thus, the negative relationship of unionization with R&D investment and productivity growth may overstate the causal impact of union coverage.

The issue of union endogeneity cannot easily be resolved with available data and techniques. Problems emanating from the nonrepresentative distribution of union coverage across sectors is largely controlled, however, by the inclusion of detailed firm and industry control variables. For example, highly unionized firms are more likely to be in less profitable, slower-growing industries with lower rates of new investment and productivity growth. In order to avoid overstating the effect of unions on firm performance, conclusions expressed in this monograph are based on regression results from specifications including 2-digit (and sometimes 3- or 4-digit) industry dummies, and industry-level variables measuring union density, sales growth, concentration, import penetration, and (in the productivity growth model) energy costs. Although the magnitude of the union coefficients are often sensitive to inclusion of industry-level variables, sizable union effects on profitability and investment behavior remain after accounting for measurable firm and industry differences.

A potentially serious qualification of the results stems from selection bias engendered by the inability to observe firms that do not survive over time. If unions decrease profitability, investment, and growth, union companies able to partially offset these effects through higher productivity or special firm advantages are more likely to survive than the average company that becomes unionized (moreover, successful firms are more likely to be targets of union organizing). For this reason, estimated negative effects of unions on profits, investment, productivity, and productivity growth are likely to understate average union effects, since firms most adversely affected by unions are least likely to have survived and be included in any sample of firms.

In addition, the absence of data on changes in firm-level union coverage over time makes it difficult to analyze the dynamic relationship between outcomes in labor, financial, investment, and product markets. And even if such data were available, modeling and measurement of these complex relationships would be difficult owing to the long-term employment relation that characterizes internal labor markets, and the long-range planning and life span of fixed R&D and physical capital.

A final, albeit rather different, concern is that expenditures on R&D and estimated R&D stocks may be inadequate proxies for the much broader category of investment—innovative activity—for which we would like to make inferences. While evidence in this area is limited, that which exists suggests that the union effects we have uncovered apply to innovative activity broadly, and not just to R&D. In work not shown in this paper, use of patent stock data instead of R&D (i.e., an output rather than an input measure of innovative activity) produced highly similar inferences about union effects. In other studies, Hirsch and Link (1987) analyze survey data from small- and medium-sized firms and find that unionized firms rank product innovative activity as being significantly less important in their strategy and performance (relative to their competitors) than do similar nonunion firms. And Acs and Audretsch (1988) find that both small- and large-firm innovations, defined according to measured outcomes independent of R&D or patents, have been significantly lower in more highly unionized industries.

Implications for the Future

The poor economic performance of unionized U.S. companies during the 1970s is likely to have played a role in the increased management resistance to union organizing and the marked contraction of the union sector during the 1980s. As indicated in the previous section, however, further study of the relationship of union coverage with economic performance is needed. First, analysis of the performance of union and nonunion companies during a more current period is essential. It is certainly possible that negative union effects on firm performance have been partially mitigated in the 1980s, owing to management and union response both to the forces of domestic and foreign competition and to the poor performance outcomes in the past. But to date, we know little about current union-nonunion differences in economic performance. Such knowledge is a prerequisite for addressing intelligently the policy debate over the appropriate role for U.S. labor law, and for understanding more clearly the transformation taking place in the workplace and in labor-management relations.

More specific issues should also be addressed in future research. Substantial interindustry differences are found in union effects on wages, profits, market value, R&D investment, capital investment, productivity, and productivity growth. Explanations for these differences across industries in relative union-nonunion outcomes, as well as an improved knowledge of the integrated relationship among the different outcome measures, would mark an important step in improving our understanding of what unions do. Further study of the complex links between labor relations, firm governance structures, and economic performance is required if we are ever to glimpse inside the black box and understand the mechanisms through which unions impact the workplace. Finally, the dynamic relationship between corporate restructuring (e.g., mergers, leveraged buyouts, and downsizing), unionization, and economic performance warrants detailed study, although this topic extends well beyond our capabilities given currently available data.

Debate over the appropriate role for U.S. labor law hinges crucially on the role of unions in the workplace and union-nonunion differences in economic performance. Weiler (1983, 1984) and others have argued that changes in National Labor Relations Board (NLRB) interpretation of labor law, the increased number of unfair labor practices, and strategic management behavior intended to avoid union organizing have seriously eroded workers' right to organize. Implicit (and sometimes explicit) in these analyses is the belief or contention that union effects in the workplace are largely benign.

An alternative interpretation (see Flanagan 1987; Freeman and Kleiner 1990) is that increased management resistance to unions and the increase in labor litigation reflects profit-maximizing behavior by employers and is due in no small part to high union wage premiums, rather than to explicit changes in labor law or in their interpretation and enforcement. The analysis in this monograph lends credence to this latter interpretation. Evidence of the poor economic performance by union companies supports the proposition that the restructuring in industrial relations and increased resistance to union organizing have been a predictable response on the part of U.S. businesses to increased domestic and foreign competition. In the absence of narrowing union-nonunion performance differences, modifications in labor law that substantially enhance union organizing and bargaining power are likely to bring about a reduced competitiveness of U.S. firms.

Labor unions are at a crucial juncture in their history. Increased foreign competition and deregulation of highly unionized domestic industries have denied unionized companies access to rents and quasi-rents that have traditionally been shared by workers and shareholders. Current rates of new union organizing are not sufficient to offset the attrition of existing union jobs, leading to a continuing decrease in the extent of union coverage in the economy. Faced with new and more severe economic constraints, union leaders and rank-and-file have been relatively slow to adjust their expectations, strategies, and wage demands. Stated more bluntly, large union concessions would have been necessary to maintain union coverage at pre-1980 levels. It is not surprising that such substantial changes in union behavior have been slow in coming (for evidence, see Freeman 1986; Curme and Macpherson, forthcoming), particularly given the importance of senior members in union decision-making. It need not follow, however, that substantial changes in union behavior and the U.S. industrial relations system will not emerge.

An implication of this study's findings is that if unions are to maintain membership at close to current levels, they must provide services that workers value, while at the same time not placing companies at a disadvantage relative to nonunion competitors (or, stated alternatively, not decreasing rates of return relative to alternative investment paths).

Union enhancement of workplace communication and labor productivity can make possible union compensation increases without concomitant decreases in firm market value. But given the rather weak relationship that currently exists between unionization and productivity, combined with strong management resistance to union organizing, the possibilities for substantial union-induced improvements in workplace productivity appear meager. It is therefore likely that we will see a continued decline in union coverage in the U.S. until a new steady-state is reached at a lower but sustainable level of union density. The size of the decline will depend on the magnitude of union effects on firm performance. If the union-nonunion differences in economic performance found for the 1970s have continued during the 1980s and beyond, the size of the union sector will continue to decline. On the other hand, a substantial diminution of union-nonunion differences in profitability, investment behavior, productivity, and growth will allow unions to survive and continue to play an important, albeit reduced, role in the U.S. labor market.

NOTES

1. Linneman and Wachter (1986), Freeman (1988), and, most convincingly, Linneman, Wachter, and Carter (1990) argue that part of the decline in union employment resulted from an increasing union wage premium in the late 1970s (see Blanchflower and Freeman, forthcoming, for international evidence). This explanation is, of course, complementary to the one offered here. An increasing wage differential, if not offset by a price or productivity increase leads to a lower profit rate. Ultimately, employment, investment, and output decisions will be based on comparative profitability or expected rates of return, and not on the wage differential per se. In work not shown, the change in company union coverage between 1977 and 1987 was found to be positively, but insignificantly, related to 1968-1980 company profitability, measured by the coefficients on firm dummies obtained in the first-step π_k equation (see chapter 4).

2. Unions may be more likely to organize in capital-intensive firms owing to greater benefits associated with collective voice in highly structured team production settings with long-lived employer-employee relationships. For fuller discussion and evidence on unionization and capital intensity, see Hirsch and Berger (1984) and Duncan and Stafford (1980).

Data Appendix 1
Variable Means by Union Category, 1968-1980

Variable	All Firms		Nonunion		Low Union		Medium Union		High Union	
	n	mean	n	mean	n	mean	n	mean	n	mean
UN	7,727	0.333	1,633	0.000	1,990	0.141	2,305	0.454	1,799	0.692
q	7,456	1.358	1,573	2.340	1,928	1.410	2,205	0.992	1,750	0.880
π_k	7,457	0.083	1,581	0.103	1,925	0.089	2,204	0.075	1,747	0.069
R&D$_1$/S	4,693	0.025	1,049	0.053	1,270	0.022	1,453	0.016	921	0.013
R&D$_2$/S	7,727	0.015	1,632	0.034	1,990	0.014	2,305	0.010	1,799	0.007
PAT/S	6,802	0.060	1,381	0.130	1,772	0.052	2,122	0.046	1,527	0.025
INV/S	7,513	0.062	1,594	0.066	1,946	0.067	2,212	0.057	1,761	0.061
ADV/S	3,879	0.020	958	0.024	1,029	0.026	1,034	0.017	858	0.015
K/L	7,270	30.277	1,521	19.878	1,891	32.868	2,154	35.165	1,704	30.506
EMPLY	7,324	21.799	1,528	10.376	1,912	19.178	2,163	26.875	1,721	28.471
DEBT/EQUITY	7,425	0.435	1,573	0.340	1,917	0.497	2,200	0.450	1,735	0.431
log(VA/L)	7,173	2.995	1,489	3.032	1,867	3.035	2,130	2.979	1,687	2.939
$\varrho_{t,t-4}$	4,616	0.025	910	0.057	1,216	0.027	1,393	0.014	1,097	0.012
I-CR4	7,727	38.899	1,633	37.200	1,990	39.455	2,305	40.482	1,799	37.797
I-DOMSH	7,727	93.398	1,633	93.053	1,990	94.731	2,305	93.250	1,799	92.427
I-GROWTH	7,727	3.379	1,633	4.866	1,990	4.101	2,305	2.798	1,799	1.972

Nonunion (UN=0); Low Union (0<UN≤.30); Medium Union (.30≤UN<.60); High Union (UN≥.60).

UN Proportion of firm's workforce covered by collective bargaining agreement.

q Tobin's q; firm market value divided by replacement cost of tangible assets.

π_k	Gross rate of return to capital; gross cash flows divided by the value of the gross inflation-adjusted capital stock.
$R\&D_1/S$	Annual R&D expenditures divided by sales, R&D-active firms only.
$R\&D_2/S$	Annual R&D expenditures divided by sales, sample includes nonreporting firms with R&D/S set to zero.
PAT/S	Patents granted per year, divided by sales (in millions of 1972$).
INV/S	Annual investment expenditures divided by sales.
ADV/S	Annual advertising expenditures divided by sales, advertising-active firms only.
K/L	Net inflation-adjusted capital stock divided by employees (thousands 1972$).
EMPLY	Employees, in thousands.
DEBT/EQUITY	Value of long-term debt adjusted for age structure, divided by equity value.
log(VA/L)	Log of value added (thousands of 1972$), divided by employees (see chapter 6).
$\varrho_{t,\,t-4}$	Annualized partial productivity growth rate, years t to $t-4$ (see text).
I-CR4	Four-firm concentration ratio in firm's primary 4-digit industry.
I-DOMSH	Percentage shipments by domestic firms in firm's primary 4-digit industry.
I-GROWTH	Annualized percentage growth rate in real industry shipments, years t to $t-4$, in firm's primary 4-digit industry.

128

Data Appendix 2
Regression Variable Definitions

UN	Proportion of firm's workforce covered by a collective bargaining agreement in 1977.
UN-LOW	Equals $1(0 < \text{UN} \le .30)$, 0 otherwise.
UN-MED	Equals 1 if $(.30 \le \text{UN} < .60)$, 0 otherwise.
UN-HIGH	Equals 1 if $(\text{UN} \ge .60)$, 0 otherwise.
UN-DUM	Equals 1 if $(\text{UN} \ge .10)$, 0 otherwise.
$\log(q)$	Log of Tobin's q, where q is the market value of the firm divided by replacement cost of tangible assets, the latter proxied by the value of the net inflation-adjusted capital stock (Cummins et al. 1985).
π_k	Gross rate of return on capital; gross cash flows divided by the net inflation-adjusted capital stock.
$\log(\text{INV})$	Log of annual capital expenditures in millions of 1972 dollars, deflated by industry deflator adjusted for fiscal year.
$\log(\text{R\&D})$	Log of annual R&D expenditures in millions of 1972 dollars, deflated by index shown in Cummins et al. (1985).
$\log(VA/L)$	Log of value added per employee, in thousands of 1972 dollars. Value added approximated by (sales – cost of goods + labor costs), the latter estimated by $[((1 + .25 \text{ UN}) \times \text{average industry compensation}) \times \text{EMPLY}]$ where data on firm's labor compensation and pension payments not available.
$\varrho_{t,t-4}$	Partial productivity growth, calculated as the annualized growth rate in value added between years t and $t-4$, minus the growth rate in employment times labor's share of value added (firms assigned labor's share based on labor costs as defined above, using midpoint of four-year period).
$\log(\text{R\&D-STK})$	Log of R&D stock in millions of 1972 dollars; calculated based on R&D expenditures and assumed 15 percent depreciation rate (Body and Jaffe, no date). Deflator shown in Cummins et al. (1985).
$\log(\text{R\&D-STK})(-1)$	Log of R&D stock minus current R&D expenditure, in millions of 1972 dollars. Calculated only for firms with reported stocks.
$\log(\text{R\&D-STK})^{\text{est}}$	Log of R&D stock in millions of 1972 dollars; actual values used for companies with reported stocks and predicted values for other companies (see text).
$\log(\text{R\&D-STK}^{\text{est}}/L)$	Measured by $\log(\text{R\&D-STK})^{\text{est}}$ minus $\log(L)$.

R&D-STK/S	R&D stock, divided by sales.
R&D-STK/S^{est}	R&D stock, divided by sales; actual values for companies with reported stocks and predicted values for other companies (see text).
log(L)	Log of employment, in thousands.
log(K)	Log of net inflation-adjusted capital stock, in millions of 1972 dollars, deflated by GNP investment implicit price deflator.
log(K)(−1)	Log of net inflation-adjusted capital stock minus current investment expenditures, in millions of 1972 dollars.
log(K/L)	Log of net inflation-adjusted capital stock per employee, in thousands of 1972 dollars.
GROWTH	Annualized growth rate in real company sales over the previous two years; sales deflated by industry-specific price indices.
I-GROWTH	Annualized percentage growth rate in real industry shipments between years t and $t-4$ in firm's primary 4-digit industry. Shipments deflated by industry-specific price indices.
I-CR4	Four-firm concentration ratio in firm's primary 4-digit industry, adjusted for regional markets and imports, available for 1972 and 1977. Pre-1972 data assigned 1972 values; post-1977 data assiged 1977 values; 1973-1976 data assigned values based on linear interpolation.
I-DOMSH	Domestic firms' percentage share of sales in firm's primary 4-digit industry, defined as 100(1− [IMPORTS/(SHIPMENTS + IMPORTS−EXPORTS)]), available for 1972 and 1977. Pre-1972 data assigned 1972 values; post-1977 data assigned 1977 values; 1973-1976 data assigned values based on linear interpolation.
I-UN	Proportion of eligible workers who are union members in firm's primary 2- or 3-digit industry during 1976-1978.
I-log(EARN)	Log of payroll per employee in firm's primary 4-digit industry, in 1972 dollars, deflated by GNP implicit price deflator.
I-ENERGY/VA	The proportion of energy costs to value added in the firm's primary 4-digit industry.

NOTE: In table 6.3, variables with "d" in front represent logarithmic differences between years t and $t-4$, divided by 4. Variables with "bars" on top represent mean values of years t and $t-4$.

REFERENCES

Abowd, John M. "The Effects of Differential Unionization Environments on the Pattern of Interindustry Investment." Cornell University. Mimeo. June 1989a.

————. "The Effect of Wage Bargains on the Stock Market Value of the Firm." *American Economic Review* 79 (September 1989b): 774-800.

Acs, Zoltan J. and David B. Audretsch. "Innovation in Large and Small Firms: An Empirical Analysis." *American Economic Review* 78 (September 1988): 678-90.

Addison, John T. and Barry T. Hirsch. "Union Effects on Productivity, Profits, and Growth: Has the Long Run Arrived?" *Journal of Labor Economics* 7 (January 1989): 72-105.

Akerlof, George A. "Labor Contracts as Partial Gift Exchange." *Quarterly Journal of Economics* 97 (November 1982): 543-69.

Allen, Steven G. "Unionization and Productivity in Office Building and School Construction." *Industrial and Labor Relations Review* 39 (January 1986): 187-201.

————. "Can Union Labor Ever Cost Less?" *Quarterly Journal of Economics* 102 (May 1987): 347-73.

Baldwin, Carliss Y. "Productivity and Labor Unions: An Application of the Theory of Self-Enforcing Contracts." *Journal of Business* 56 (April 1983): 155-85.

Becker, Brian E. "Concession Bargaining: The Impact on Shareholders' Equity." *Industrial and Labor Relations Review* 40 (January 1987): 268-79.

Becker, Brian E. and Craig A. Olson. "Labor Relations and Firm Performance." In M. Kleiner, R. Block, M. Roomkin, and S. Salsburg, *Human Resources and the Performance of the Firm.* Madison: Industrial Relations Research Association, 1987.

————. "Unionization and Shareholder Interests." *Industrial and Labor Relations Review* 42 (January 1989): 246-61.

————. "Unionization and Firm Profits." SUNY-Buffalo and University of Wisconsin, Mimeo. January 1990.

Blanchflower, David G. and Richard B. Freeman. "Going Different Ways: Unionism in the U.S. and Other O.E.C.D. Countries." In M.F. Bognanno and M.M. Kleiner, *The Future Roles of Unions, Industry and Government in Industrial Relations,* conference volume to be published in *Industrial Relations* (forthcoming).

Body, David and Adam Jaffe. "Documentation for Data Set SPV." National Bureau of Economic Research. Mimeo. No date.

Bound, John, Clint Cummins, Zvi Griliches, Bronwyn H. Hall, and Adam Jaffe. "Who Does R&D and Who Patents?" In Zvi Griliches (ed.), *R&D, Patents, and Productivity.* Chicago: University of Chicago Press, 1984.

Bothwell, James L., Thomas F. Cooley, and Thomas E. Hall. "A New View of the Market Structure-Performance Debate." *Journal of Industrial Economics* 32 (June 1984): 397-417.

Bronars, Stephen G. and Donald R. Deere. "Union Rent-Sharing and Firm Behavior." University of California, Santa Barbara and Texas A&M. Mimeo. June 1989.

_____. "Union Representation Elections and Firm Profitability." *Industrial Relations* 29 (Winter 1990): 15-37.

_____. "The Threat of Unionization, the Use of Debt, and the Preservation of Shareholder Wealth." *Quarterly Journal of Economics* 106 (February 1991): 231-254.

Bronars, Stephen G., Donald R. Deere, and Joseph Tracy. "The Prevalence and Effects of Differences in Unionization Among Firms in the Same Output Market." University of California, Santa Barbara, Texas A&M, and Yale. Mimeo. October 1989.

Brown, Charles and James Medoff. "Trade Unions in the Production Process." *Journal of Political Economy* 86 (June 1978): 355-78.

Brown, James N. and Orley Ashenfelter. "Testing the Efficiency of Employment Contracts." *Journal of Political Economy* 94 (June 1986, supplement): S40-S87.

Card, David. "Efficient Contracts with Costly Adjustment: Short-Run Employment Determination for Airline Mechanics." *American Economic Review* 76 (December 1986): 1045-71.

Chaison, Gary N. and Dileep G. Dhavale. "A Note on the Severity of the Decline in Union Organizing Activity." *Industrial and Labor Relations Review* 43 (April 1990): 366-73.

Clark, Kim B. "The Impact of Unionization on Productivity: A Case Study." *Industrial and Labor Relations Review* 33 (July 1980a): 451-69.

_____. "Unionization and Productivity: Micro-Econometric Evidence." *Quarterly Journal of Economics* 95 (December 1980b): 613-39.

_____. "Unionization and Firm Performance: The Impact on Profits, Growth, and Productivity." *American Economic Review* 74 (December 1984): 893-919.

Connolly, Robert A., Barry T. Hirsch, and Mark Hirschey. "Union Rent Seeking, Intangible Capital, and Market Value of the Firm." *Review of Economics and Statistics* 68 (November 1986): 567-77.

Crawford, Vincent. "Long-Term Relationships Governed by Short-Term Contracts." *American Economic Review* 78 (June 1988): 485-499.

Cummins, Clint, Bronwyn H. Hall, Elizabeth S. Laderman, and Joy Mundy. "The R&D Master File: Documentation." National Bureau of Economic Research. Mimeo. September 1985.

Curme, Michael A., Barry T. Hirsch, and David A. Macpherson. "Union Membership and Contract Coverage in the United States, 1983-1988." *Industrial and Labor Relations Review* 44 (October 1990): 5-33.

Curme, Michael A. and David A. Macpherson. "Union Wage Differentials and the Effects of Industry and Local Union Density." *Journal of Labor Research* (forthcoming).

Dickens, William T. and Jonathan S. Leonard. "Accounting for the Decline in Union Membership, 1950-1980." *Industrial and Labor Relations Review* 38 (April 1985): 323-34.

Domowitz, Ian, R. Glenn Hubbard, and Bruce C. Petersen. "The Intertemporal Stability of the Concentration-Margins Relationship." *Journal of Industrial Economics* 35 (September 1986): 13-34.

Duncan, Greg J. and Frank P. Stafford. "Do Union Members Receive Compensating Wage Differentials?" *American Economic Review* 70 (June 1980): 355-71.

Eberts, Randall W. and Joe A. Stone. "On the Contract Curve: A Test of Alternative Models of Collective Bargaining." *Journal of Labor Economics* 4 (January 1986): 66-81.

Farber, Henry S. "The Analysis of Union Behavior." In Orley Ashenfelter and Richard Layard (eds.), *Handbook of Labor Economics, Volume II.* Amsterdam: North-Holland, 1986.

Flanagan, Robert J., *Labor Relations and the Litigation Explosion.* Washington: Brookings Institution, 1987.

Foulkes, Fred K. *Personnel Policies in Large Nonunion Companies.* Englewood Cliffs, NJ: Prentice-Hall, 1980.

Freeman, Richard B. "Individual Mobility and Union Voice in the Labor Market." *American Economic Review Papers and Proceedings* 66 (May 1976): 361-68.

_____. "Unionism, Price-Cost Margins, and the Return to Capital." National Bureau of Economic Research Working Paper No. 1164, July 1983.

_____. "Longitudinal Analyses of the Effects of Trade Unions." *Journal of Labor Economics* 2 (January 1984): 1-26.

_____. "Why Are Unions Faring Poorly in NLRB Representation Elections?" In Thomas A. Kochan (ed.), *Challenges and Choices Facing American Labor.* Cambridge: MIT Press, 1985.

_____. "In Search of Union Wage Concessions in Standard Data Sets." *Industrial Relations* 25 (Spring 1986): 131-145.

_____. "Contraction and Expansion: The Divergence of Private Sector and Public Sector Unionism in the United States." *Journal of Economic Perspectives* 2 (Spring 1988): 63-88.

Freeman, Richard B. and Morris M. Kleiner. "Employer Behavior in the Face of Union Organizing Drives." *Industrial and Labor Relations Review* 43 (April 1990): 351-65.

Freeman, Richard B. and James L. Medoff. *What Do Unions Do?* New York: Basic Books, 1984.

Griliches, Zvi (ed.). *R&D, Patents, and Productivity.* Chicago: University of Chicago Press, 1984.

_____. "Productivity, R&D, and Basic Research at the Firm Level in the 1970's." *American Economic Review* 76 (March 1986): 141-54.

Griliches, Zvi and Jerry A. Hausman. "Errors in Variables in Panel Data." *Journal of Econometrics* 31 (February 1986): 93-118.

Grout, Paul A. "Investment and Wages in the Absence of Binding Contracts: A Nash Bargaining Approach." *Econometrica* 52 (March 1984): 449-60.

Hausman, Jerry A. "Specification Tests in Econometrics." *Econometrica* 46 (November 1978): 1251-71.

Hirsch, Barry T. "Innovative Activity, Productivity Growth, and Firm Performance: Are Labor Unions a Spur or a Deterrent?" *Advances in Applied Micro-Economics,* Vol. 5. Greenwich, CT: JAI Press, 1990a, 69-104.

_____. "Market Structure, Union Rent Seeking, and Firm Profitability." *Economics Letters* 32 (1990b): 75-79.

_____. "Union Coverage and Profitability among U.S. Firms," *Review of Economics and Statistics* 73 (May 1991).

_____. "Firm Investment Behavior and Collective Bargaining Strategy." In M.F. Bognanno and M.M. Kleiner, *The Future Roles of Unions, Industry and Government in Industrial Relations,* conference volume to be published in *Industrial Relations* (forthcoming).

Hirsch, Barry T. and John T. Addison. *The Economic Analysis of Unions: New Approaches and Evidence.* Boston: Allen & Unwin, 1986.

Hirsch, Barry T. and Mark C. Berger. "Union Membership Determination and Industry Characteristics." *Southern Economic Journal* 50 (January 1984): 665-79.

Hirsch, Barry T. and Robert A. Connolly. "Do Unions Capture Monopoly Profits?" *Industrial and Labor Relations Review* 41 (October 1987): 118-36.

Hirsch, Barry T. and Albert N. Link. "Unions, Productivity, and Productivity Growth." *Journal of Labor Research* 5 (Winter 1984): 29-37.

_____. "Labor Union Effects on Innovative Activity." *Journal of Labor Research* 8 (Fall 1987): 323-32.

Hirsch, Barry T. and Terry G. Seaks. "Functional Form in Regression Models of Tobin's q." University of North Carolina at Greensboro. Mimeo. July 1990.

Ichniowski, Casey. "Ruling Out Productivity? Labor Contract Pages and Plant Performance." National Bureau of Economic Research Working Paper No. 1368, June 1984.

Ippolito, Richard A. "The Economic Function of Underfunded Pension Plans." *Journal of Law and Economics* 28 (October 1985): 611-51.

_____. "A Study of the Regulatory Effect of the Employee Retirement Income Security Act." *Journal of Law and Economics* 31 (April 1988): 85-125.

Karier, Thomas. "Unions and Monopoly Profits." *Review of Economics and Statistics* 67 (February 1985): 34-42.

Kazis, Richard. "Rags to Riches? One Industry's Strategy for Improving Productivity." *Technology Review* (August/September 1989): 43-53.

Klein, Benjamin, Robert G. Crawford, and Armen A. Alchian. "Vertical Integration, Appropriable Rents, and the Competitive Contracting Process." *Journal of Law and Economics* 21 (October 1978): 297-326.

Kochan, Thomas A., Harry C. Katz, and Robert B. McKersie. *The Transformation of American Industrial Relations.* New York: Basic Books, 1986.

Kokkelenberg, Edward C. and Donna R. Sockell. "Union Membership in the United States, 1973-1981." *Industrial and Labor Relations Review* 38 (July 1985): 497-543.

Kruse, Douglas L. "Essays on Profit-Sharing and Unemployment." Unpublished doctoral dissertation, Harvard University, May 1988.

Lach, Saul and Mark Schankerman. "Dynamics of R&D and Investment in the Scientific Sector." *Journal of Political Economy* 97 (August 1989): 880-904.

Lawrence, Colin and Robert Z. Lawrence. "Manufacturing Wage Dispersion: An End Game Interpretation." *Brookings Papers on Economic Activity* (1:1985): 47-106.

Lazear, Edward P. "A Competitive Theory of Monopoly Unionism." *American Economic Review* 73 (September 1983): 631-43.

Leonard, Jonathan S. "Unions and Employment Growth." In M.F. Bognanno and M.M. Kleiner, *The Future Roles of Unions, Industry and Government in Industrial Relations,* conference volume to be published in *Industrial Relations* (forthcoming).

Levin, Richard C., Alvin K. Klevorick, Richard R. Nelson, and Sidney G. Winter. "Appropriating the Returns from Industrial Research and Development." *Brookings Papers on Economic Activity* (3:1987): 783-820.

Linneman, Peter D. and Michael L. Wachter. "Rising Union Premiums and the Declining Boundaries Among Noncompeting Groups." *American Economic Review Papers and Proceedings* 76 (May 1986): 103-08.

Linneman, Peter D., Michael L. Wachter, and William H. Carter. "Evaluating the Evidence on Union Employment and Wages." *Industrial and Labor Relations Review* 44 (October 1990):34-53.

MaCurdy, Thomas E. and John H. Pencavel. "Testing Between Competing Models of Wage and Employment Determination in Unionized Markets." *Journal of Political Economy* 94 (June 1986, supplement): S3-S39.

Metcalf, David. "Trade Unions and Economic Performance: The British Evidence." Discussion Paper No. 320, Centre for Labour Economics, London School of Economics, August 1988.

Ploeg, F. van der. "Trade Unions, Investment, and Employment: A Noncooperative Approach." *European Economic Review* 31 (October 1987): 1465-92.

Ravenscraft, David J. "Structure-Profit Relationships at the Line of Business and Industry Level." *Review of Economics and Statistics* 65 (February 1983): 22-31.

Reder, Melvin W. "The Rise and Fall of Unions: The Public Sector and the Private." *Journal of Economic Perspectives* 2 (Spring 1988): 89-110.

Reder, Melvin W. and George R. Neumann. "Conflict and Contract: The Case of Strikes." *Journal of Political Economy* 88 (October 1980): 867-86.

Rosen, Sherwin. "Trade Union Power, Threat Effects and the Extent of Organization." *Review of Economic Studies* 36 (April 1969): 185-96.

Ruback, Richard S. and Martin B. Zimmerman. "Unionization and Profitability: Evidence from the Capital Market." *Journal of Political Economy* 92 (December 1984): 1134-57.

Salinger, Michael A. "Tobin's q, Unionization, and the Concentration-Profits Relationship." *Rand Journal of Economics* 15 (Summer 1984): 159-70.

Svejnar, Jan. "Bargaining Power, Fear of Disagreement, and Wage Settlements: Theory and Evidence From U.S. Industry." *Econometrica* 54 (September 1986): 1055-78.

Tauman, Y. and Y. Weiss. "Labor Unions and the Adoption of New Technology." *Journal of Labor Economics* 5 (October 1987): 477-501.

Troy, Leo and Neil Sheflin. *Union Sourcebook: Membership, Structure, Finance, Directory,* First Edition. West Orange, NJ: Industrial Relations Data and Information Services, 1985.

U.S. Bureau of the Census. *Statistical Abstract of the United States: 1989,* 109th ed. Washington, DC, January 1989.

Verma, Anil. "Relative Flow of Capital to Union and Nonunion Plants Within a Firm," *Industrial Relations* 24 (Fall 1985): 395-405.

Voos, Paula B. and Lawrence R. Mishel. "The Union Impact on Profits: Evidence from Industry Price-Cost Margin Data." *Journal of Labor Economics* 4 (January 1986): 105-33.

Wachter, Michael L. and George M. Cohen. "The Law and Economics of Collective Bargaining: An Introduction and Application to the Problems of Subcontracting, Partial Closure, and Relocation." *University of Pennsylvania Law Review* 136 (May 1988): 1349-417.

Weiler, Paul. "Promises to Keep: Securing Workers' Rights to Self-Organization under the NLRA." *Harvard Law Review* 96 (June 1983): 1769-827.

_____. "Striking a New Balance: Freedom of Contract and the Prospects for Union Representation." *Harvard Law Review* 98 (December 1984): 351-420.

Weiss, Leonard W. and George A. Pascoe, Jr. "Adjusted Concentration Ratios in Manufacturing, 1972 and 1977." Statistical Report of the Bureau of Economics to the Federal Trade Commission, June 1986.

Wessels, Walter J. "The Effects of Unions on Employment and Productivity: An Unresolved Contradiction." *Journal of Labor Economics* 3 (January 1985): 101-08.

Williamson, Oliver E., Michael L. Wachter, and Jeffrey E. Harris. "'Understanding the Employment Relation: The Analysis of Idiosyncratic Exchange." *Bell Journal of Economics* 6 (Spring 1975): 250-78.

INDEX